# TOP **10**
# PRAGUE

T0286262

# CONTENTS

**4**

## Introducing Prague

| | |
|---|---|
| Welcome to Prague | 6 |
| The Story of Prague | 8 |
| Top 10 Experiences | 12 |
| Itineraries | 14 |

**18**

## Top 10 Highlights

| | |
|---|---|
| Explore the Highlights | 20 |
| Prague Castle | 22 |
| St Vitus Cathedral | 26 |
| Old Town Square | 28 |
| Charles Bridge | 32 |
| Loreta | 34 |
| Jewish Museum | 36 |
| St Agnes of Bohemia Convent | 40 |
| Wenceslas Square | 42 |
| National Museum | 44 |
| Petřín Hill | 46 |

## 48

# Top 10 of Everything

| | |
|---|---|
| Churches | 50 |
| Historical Sites | 52 |
| Museums and Galleries | 54 |
| Writers and Composers | 56 |
| House Signs | 58 |
| Myths and Legends | 60 |
| Eccentric Prague | 64 |
| Parks and Gardens | 66 |
| Off the Beaten Track | 68 |
| Family Attractions | 70 |
| Performing Arts Venues | 72 |
| Nights Out | 74 |
| Prague Dishes | 76 |
| Bars and Kavárnas | 78 |
| Shops and Markets | 80 |
| Prague for Free | 82 |
| Festivals | 84 |

## 86

# Area by Area

| | |
|---|---|
| Staré Město | 88 |
| Malá Strana | 96 |
| Prague Castle and Hradčany | 104 |
| Josefov and Northern Staré Město | 112 |
| Nové Město | 118 |
| Greater Prague | 126 |

## 134

# Streetsmart

| | | | |
|---|---|---|---|
| Getting Around | 136 | Index | 148 |
| Practical Information | 140 | Phrase Book | 156 |
| Places to Stay | 144 | Acknowledgments | 158 |

# PRAGUE

# INTRODUCING

Welcome to Prague 6

The Story of Prague 8

Top 10 Experiences 12

Itineraries 14

*Charles Bridge illuminated at sunset*

# WELCOME TO
# **PRAGUE**

**Prague has firmly established itself as one of Europe's most popular cities, where Art Nouveau masterpieces line medieval streets and the planet's best beer is enjoyed on Baroque squares. Don't want to miss a thing? With Top 10 Prague, you'll enjoy the very best the city has to offer.**

The City of a Hundred Spires, Prague has a way of enchanting everyone who strolls its cobbled lanes. It's been fortunate enough over the centuries to have escaped both extensive war damage and the makeovers of over-zealous urban planners. The result? A central core that has changed little since the 14th century, when Prague was the capital of the Holy Roman Empire. A stroll past the Gothic and Baroque buildings on the Old Town Square is to wind back the centuries, the Old Town Hall's Astronomical Clock still chiming by the hour as you follow the coronation route of the

**Overlooking the Vltava river**

Bohemian kings over Charles Bridge up to Prague Castle. Pretty buildings are Prague's DNA; you never have to walk too far to stumble upon epic cathedrals like St Vitus or fairytale churches like Loreta. And the city's rich history doesn't stop there, with the snaggletooth headstones of the Old Jewish Cemetery testifying to the city's once thriving Jewish community.

Prague is a historic city through and through, but to focus too much on the past is to overlook all that the city offers today. For starters, there's the world-class beer scene, where a dewy half-litre of golden Czech lager or a mug of Pilsner Urquell might well be the best – and some of the

cheapest – beer in the world. Then there's the art scene, with David Černý's darkly humorous public art making the city an open-air gallery, and the epic National Gallery showcasing modern pieces across multiple locations. Better still, Prague has enough green spaces to make you forget all about bridges and castles, from the lush slopes of Petřín Hill to former monastery orchards.

So, where to start? With Top 10 Prague, of course. This pocket-sized guide gets to the heart of the city with simple lists of ten, expert local knowledge and comprehensive maps, helping you turn an ordinary trip into an extraordinary one.

# THE STORY OF
# **PRAGUE**

Prague's story is a turbulent tale. What began as a castle on a rocky outcrop would rise to become the seat of an empire before declining into a backwater of the Habsburg Empire. In the 20th century alone it assumed numerous identities before eventually becoming the capital of the Czech Republic. And yet, despite the setbacks, the city has risen again, stronger after each fall. Here's the story of how it came to be.

## Prague Begins

Evidence of human activity here dates back to the Paleolithic era, but it wasn't until the 4th century BCE that Celtic tribes built settlements around modern-day Prague. Germanic tribes followed in the 1st century BCE with the first Slavs arriving in the 6th century CE. These new arrivals clashed with the existing tribes and their struggles led to the emergence of the first ruling Slavic dynasty of the Bohemian region, the Přemyslid dynasty, in around 800. They consolidated their position by constructing fortified settlements at Vyšehrad and where Prague Castle stands today; these buildings marked the foundation of Prague. Thanks to the security offered by these fortifications, the settlements grew and prospered, and in 950, the Bohemian Kingdom was subsumed into the Holy Roman Empire.

## A City Emerges

Despite being one of the most powerful regions within the German-dominated Holy Roman Empire, the nascent city of Prague was still a collection of separate settlements. Only in 1172 was the first stone bridge, Judith Bridge, built across the Vltava, joining the existing villages. In the century that followed Staré Město (Old Town) and Malá Strana (the Little Quarter) were established, the latter as an area for German migrants to settle in. It was also at this time that Prague's Jews began to be confined to what would become the Jewish Ghetto.

## Seat of Empire

The Přemyslid dynasty, which ruled Prague for nearly five centuries, came to an end in 1306 with the murder of its ruler. Power was transferred to John of Luxembourg, kickstarting a golden era

**Radical Czech theologian and philosopher, Jan Hus**

that continued under his son Charles IV, who would also become Holy Roman Emperor. Charles made Prague the capital of his empire and successfully transformed it into a leading European city; he founded a university, commissioned Charles Bridge, laid out Nové Město (New Town) and commenced the construction of St Vitus Cathedral.

## Religious Strife

But with highs came lows. In 1389 anti-Jewish pogroms saw around 3,000 of Prague's Jews murdered. Not long after, in 1415, the radical Prague Hussite preacher Jan Hus was burned at the stake in Germany after railing against immoral practices of the church. His death instigated the Hussite wars – two decades of fighting between Protestants and Catholics that resulted in Catholic victory. In 1526, the Catholic Habsburgs became rulers of Prague and began to crush Protestantism. Their efforts led to the second defenestration in 1618, when a group of Protestant noblemen threw three Catholic officials from a window of Prague Castle. This helped spark the Thirty Years' War and the Protestant defeat in 1620 at the Battle of White Mountain, west of Prague. The result for Prague was Habsburg rule for the next 300 years and relegation from imperial capital to provincial city.

**Charles IV and the foundation stone of the Charles Bridge**

## Moments in History

### 9th century
The founding of Prague, with the first sites constructed on Vyšehrad hill.

### 1348
Bohemian king Charles IV becomes Holy Roman Emperor and makes Prague his capitcal.

### 1415
Radical Bohemian preacher Jan Hus is burned at the stake, leading to decades of religious war.

### 1618
The Defenestration at Prague Castle plays a key role in inciting the Thirty Years' War, which decimates Prague.

### 1620
The Habsburgs win the Battle of the White Mountain, near to today's airport, ending Prague's prominence within the Holy Roman Empire.

**1918**

The Independent Czechoslovakia Republic is founded at the end of World War I with Tomáš Masaryk elected as its first president.

**1939–1945**

Nazis invade and occupy Prague during World War II.

**1948**

The Czechoslovak Communist Party takes power in a coup.

**1968**

The liberal reforms of the Prague Spring are brutally crushed by a Soviet Union-led invasion.

**1989**

The student-led "Velvet Revolution" contributes to the downfall of the Communist government.

**2022–present**

Czechs welcome hundreds of thousands of Ukrainian refugees fleeing the war with Russia.

## National Revival

Things would get worse before they got better. The rest of the 17th century saw plague and a great fire in 1689. The Habsburgs used this as an opportunity to rebuild the city in Baroque style. Great new buildings, gardens and churches, including the National Theatre and Clementinum, were built in this period. The city became a hub of industrialization with a population that doubled in the 18th century and would continue to grow. In 1784, the four towns of Prague (Staré Město, Nové Město, Malá Strana and Hradčany) were merged into a single, unified city. As Prague expanded so did the collective idea of a "Czech" identity among all strata of society. The populace briefly revolted in 1848, and though this was quickly and brutally suppressed, the ruling Habsburgs began to loosen their grip in the decades that followed, thus allowing the Czech people to rediscover their history and culture.

## Czechoslovakia and World War II

Following the collapse of the Austro-Hungarian Empire in 1918, an independent Czech and Slovak state (Czechoslovakia) was founded, with Prague as its capital. The new country initially prospered both economically and culturally under the leadership of President Tomáš Masaryk, but the Great Depression and then the rise of Adolf

**Nazi leader Adolf Hitler meets a group of German students in Prague**

**President Petr Pavel with German President Frank-Walter Steinmeier**

Hitler halted such growth. Just 20 years after its foundation, Czechoslovakia was surrendered to Nazi Germany as part of the Munich Agreement. In March 1939 Prague was occupied by the Nazis. The city suffered heavily during World War II, both from Nazi persecution of its citizens, especially the Jewish population (which has never recovered), and a number of Allied bombing raids. In May 1945, Prague was liberated following a citywide uprising and the arrival of the Soviet Red Army.

## Communism and Freedom

In the first free election following the war, in 1946, the Czechoslovak Communist Party won a plurality of support from a war-weary population. Perhaps emboldened by this, the Communists consolidated power in a coup and Prague remained under the Soviet sphere of influence for the next four decades. The early years saw brutal repression as a Soviet-style dictatorship was imposed, but by the 1960s there was hope for change. This came to fruition in 1968, when Communist leader Alexander Dubček introduced a series of liberal reforms known as the "Prague Spring". The movement was ruthlessly crushed by a massive Soviet-led military invasion on 21 August 1968. The harsh rule that followed became known as the period

of "normalization" by Czechs and gave rise to an underground dissident movement of writers, actors and intellectuals who later spearheaded the 1989 "Velvet Revolution". After weeks of nationwide protests, the Communists fell to public pressure and playwright Václav Havel became president.

## Prague Today

The early years of the post-Communist transition were marked by huge political and economic shifts towards capitalism, and the peaceful split of Czechoslovakia into two states on 1 January 1993. The Czech Republic gradually integrated into Europe, joining NATO in 1999 and the European Union in 2004. Prague has also become one of Europe's biggest tourist destinations and one of its most celebrated historic cities, thanks to the preservation of its stunning medieval architecture. The past decade has seen the country become increasingly divided over immigration and face key issues related to high inflation and climate change. In December 2023 the city was shocked by a mass shooting that left 14 dead and many injured. Yet Prague has tackled these challenges head on, toughening its gun laws and introducing climate solutions. Most importantly, it remains an open city as evidenced by the roughly 500,000 Ukrainian refugees Prague has welcomed since 2022.

# TOP 10
# EXPERIENCES

Planning the perfect trip to Prague? Whether you're visiting for the first time or making a return trip, there are some things you simply shouldn't miss out on. To make the most of your time, and to enjoy the best this popular Central European capital has to offer, be sure to add these experiences to your list.

**1 See architectural marvels**
Where staggeringly beautiful buildings are concerned, Prague has an embarrassment of riches. Majestic architecture awaits on every corner, whether it's the Old Town Hall *(p30)* with its Astronomical Clock, the magnificent St Nicholas Church *(p98)* or the Baroque masterpiece that is Prague Castle *(p22)*.

**2 Enjoy highbrow culture evenings**
Classical music is the lifeblood of Prague and the opera and theatre scenes are world-class (and yet, reasonably priced). Check out the esteemed shows at the National Theatre *(p120)* or see concerts at the Rudolfinum *(p73)* or Smetana Hall at the Municipal House *(p89)*.

**3 Drink great beer**
Lift a glass of Czech beer and you'll understand why Czechs drink more of the stuff per capita than any nation on earth: the beer here is simply excellent. Join the locals for a pint of beloved local lager, Pilsner Urquell, or seek out tipples such as Únětice, Budvar and Prague's own Staropramen.

**4 Take in the view**
Prague's historic core is blessed with a crown of surrounding hills that offer breathtaking vistas over the city's shapely spires, cupolas and bridges. Snap a classic skyline photo from the hilltops of Letná Park *(p128)*, Strahov Monastery or Petřín Hill *(p46)*; they're all equally iconic.

## 5 Eat like a royal

Hearty and delicious, Czech food is about flavours and textures. Ensure you try local favourites goulash (a paprika-enriched stew) and svíčková (roast beef in a sauce). Then there's the national dish: roast pork, best served with soft dumplings to soak up that rich gravy.

## 6 Relax in parks and gardens

Tucked away behind ornate walls or flanking Renaissance palaces, Prague's historic gardens are tranquil oases. Don't miss the Baroque Palace Gardens (p67), the Renaissance Wallenstein Garden (p83) or the lovely Vrtba Garden (p99), which stretches over three ornate levels.

## 7 Catch an ice-hockey match

Many locals live for the frenetic thrill of ice-hockey, the Czech national sport. See the best players in action at the O2 Arena, where visiting teams battle with hometown HC Sparta Praha. The excitement on the ice is matched by the feverish enthusiasm in the stands.

## 8 Chill with coffee and cake

Move over Paris and Vienna: Prague's coffee culture can match any city in Europe. Relax over a perfect cappuccino in Café Slavia (p94) or sip a quick espresso in Café Louvre (p124). Pair your coffee with an apple strudel, pancakes or honey-cake (medovník).

## 9 Admire unusual art

It might be home to masterpieces of European art, but Prague also celebrates its weird side. Local shock-artist David Černý's hanging horse (p68) and rotating Kafka head are worth a visit, while the mysterious headless statue by Jaroslav Róna is a transfixing oddity.

## 10 Discover Communist History

Simply walking through Prague, passing sites such as the memorial at Petřín Hill and Žižkov TV Tower (p128), offers a primer in Communist history. For a lesson on the years of dictatorship, visit the Museum of Communism (p122).

# ITINERARIES

Seeing the Old Town Square, enjoying beer in a local pub or beer hall, visiting the ancient Prague Castle: there's a lot to see and do in Prague. With places to eat, drink or take in the view, these itineraries offer ways to spend 2 days and 4 days in the capital.

## 2 DAYS

### Day 1

#### Morning
Start your exploration of Prague at the striking Art Nouveau Municipal House (*Obecní dům, p89*) and the medieval Powder Gate (*p89*), where Bohemian kings once began their coronation route to Prague Castle. Follow in their footsteps through the gate, heading down Celetná street with its many shops and cafés until you reach the Old Town Square (*p28*). Stand at its centre to appreciate the varied architecture of the Old Town Hall, the Church of Our Lady before Týn and the Astronomical Clock – where you can see the clock's procession of the 12 Apostles.

#### Afternoon
Wander over to the Vltava river and ascend the steps of the astronomical tower of the Clementinum (*p90*), a former Jesuit college, for stunning views

>
> **DRINK**
> You're never far from a pub in the centre of town. Good options – for both a beer and a meal – include U Fleků (*p124*) and Pivovar Národní (*pivovarnarodni.cz*).

over Charles Bridge (*p32*) before a pitstop for a hearty lunch and a Pilsner at V Zátiší (*p95*). Then it's time to stroll over to the two sites of the National Museum (*p44*) at the top of the vast Wenceslas Square (*p42*). A whole afternoon can be spent exploring the history, science and kids exhibits in both the beautiful main building and the annex, which are conveniently linked by a tunnel. Finish your first day with tasty Czech dishes at Restaurace Bredovský dvůr (*p125*).

**Historic streets in the centre of Prague's Old Town**

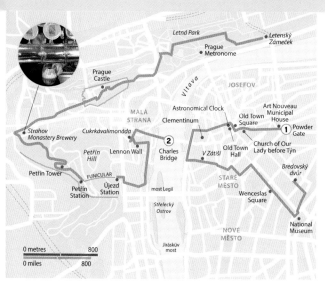

## Day 2

### Morning
Your second day is all about the other side of the river. Get up early to cross the iconic Charles Bridge (p32) before the crowds build up. Having crossed, grab coffee at Cukrkávalimonáda (p102) and meander through the quiet streets of Mála Strana – Beatles fans should pay a visit to the graffiti-clad Lennon Wall (p82). Leave the city streets behind and take the funicular up to the greenery of Petřín Hill (p46), one of Prague's largest parks, home to woodlands, beautiful gardens and a hilariously unflattering mirror maze. Be sure to take in the dramatic views down to Staré Město.

### Afternoon
Enjoy a languorous lunch at the Strahov Monastery Brewery (p108)

before tackling St Vitus Cathedral and the labyrinth of historic sights that comprises Prague Castle (p22), such as St George's Basilica, Lobkowicz Palace and Golden Lane. Spend as much time as you need soaking in the history here before heading to your final stop, Letná Park (p128). Once in Letná, make a bee-line for the towering metronome (p52) – the largest functioning metronome in the world – and Letenský zámeček restaurant (letenskyzamecek.cz) in the park's eastern end. This is the perfect spot to enjoy a meal and a well-earned drink in the beer garden as the sun sets.

> 📷 **VIEW**
> Don't pay to climb Petřín Tower – the view is just as good from the trails heading north from the tower towards Prague Castle and Strahov Monastery.

**Beer garden with a view at Letenský zámeček**

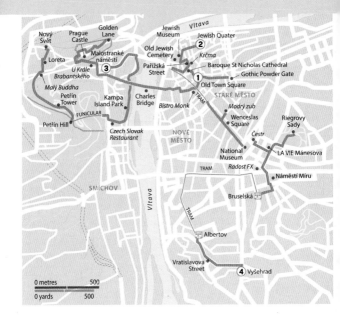

# 4 DAYS

## Day 1

There are few better places to start a trip through Prague than Staré Město. Begin with a tour of the city's architecture in the streets around Old Town Square (p28). Look out for the variety of styles on show: the medieval Gothic Powder Gate (p89), the Art Nouveau Municipal House (p89), and the Baroque St Nicholas Cathedral (p90). Soak up the lively atmosphere in the square itself with a lunch of fresh produce at Bistro Monk (p95). before you head over to Prague Castle (p22) for the afternoon, crossing the iconic Charles Bridge (p32) on the way. Learn about the castle's

**Medieval Astronomical clock on the Old Town Hall**

fascinating history at the Prague Castle Story exhibition and then pop into the castle's other sites – Golden Lane is worth seeing. End your sojourn through history with dinner at the medieval-styled U Krále Brabantského (p109).

## Day 2

Devote your morning to the historic Jewish Quarter, Josefov, beginning with

**EAT**
Don't overlook the restaurants around Old Town Square. Amid the touristy spots are hidden gems like 420 (420restaurant.cz), helmed by Michelin-starred Radek Kašpárek.

> **DRINK**
> Eschew the big name beers for the Vinohradský Pivovar micro-brewer in Vinohrady (*vinohradsky pivovar.cz*). Pair one of the beers with the brewery's tasty Czech food.

the seven sites of the Jewish Museum (*p36*). Learn about Jewish culture and history and don't miss the fascinating Old Jewish Cemetery (*p113*). Give yourself a break between each site with some retail therapy in the bespoke shops on Pařížská street, and then enjoy a lunch of classic Bohemian dishes at Krčma (*p117*). Jump on tram A at Staroměstská Můstek to leap forward in time with a visit to Wenceslas Square (*p42*), in Nové Město. Soak in the Art Nouveau palaces found around the square and then its off to the top of the square for a couple of hours in the National Museum (*p44*). home to exhibits on everything from minerals to communism. Before you leave, admire the incredible frescoes found in the entrance hall. End the day with fine Thai fare at Modrý zub (*p125*) and a drink at one of the many excellent bars that surround Wenceslas Square.

## Day 3

Today it's time to see the greener side of Prague. Start in the sprawling Malostranské Náměstí square, with its beautiful palace arcades and fabulous Baroque St Nicholas Church (*p98*). From here, you can enjoy a leisurely amble through Kampa Island park (*p98*) right on the Vltava river – look out for the oddly transfixing sculptures of faceless babies in the park – with a stop at the somewhat unimaginatively named Czech Slovak Restaurant (*p103*) for a lunch of modern Czech cuisine. Refuelled, catch the funicular to the top of Petřín Hill (*p46*) where you can enjoy an afternoon in this grand forested park. Just make sure you climb the 299 steps of Petřín Tower – a copy of the Eiffel Tower – for unsurpassed views over Prague. Afterwards, find the trail that

leads north to Loreta (*p34*) where you can dine on superb east Asian cuisine at the vegan Malý Buddha (*p109*), before a stroll along tranquil Nový Svět (*p106*).

## Day 4

Your final day is all about Prague's less-visited spots. Hop on metro line C to lofty Vyšehrad (*p127*), a fort believed to be the ancient seat of Czech princes. Explore the rotunda and cemetery, where over 600 famous Czechs are buried, before walking down sloping Vratislavova street to admire Cubist houses. Hop on tram 5 from Albertov to Bruselská and then wander over to LA VIE Mánesova for a leisurely lunch (*tekutemaso.cz*). The afternoon can then be spent exploring the shops of leafy Náměstí Míru and attractive Vinohrady. As the sun begins to dip, walk over to Riegrovy Sady park; if you're lucky, there'll be a beautiful sunset over the valley. Dine at the Čestr (*p125*) meat smokehouse and then party your last night away at Radost FX (*p123*).

**Centuries-old stairs leading down to Novy Svet**

# TOP 10 HIGHLIGHTS

| | |
|---|---|
| Explore the Highlights | 20 |
| Prague Castle | 22 |
| St Vitus Cathedral | 26 |
| Old Town Square | 28 |
| Charles Bridge | 32 |
| Loreta | 34 |
| Jewish Museum | 36 |
| St Agnes of Bohemia Convent | 40 |
| Wenceslas Square | 42 |
| National Museum | 44 |
| Petřín Hill | 46 |

*Old Town Square*

# EXPLORE THE
# HIGHLIGHTS

There are some sights in Prague you simply shouldn't miss, and it's these attractions that make the Top 10. Discover what makes each one a must-see on the following pages.

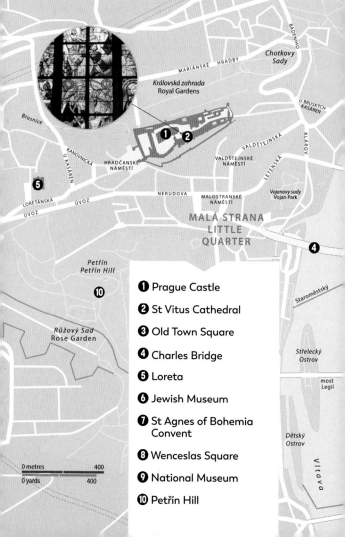

❶ Prague Castle

❷ St Vitus Cathedral

❸ Old Town Square

❹ Charles Bridge

❺ Loreta

❻ Jewish Museum

❼ St Agnes of Bohemia Convent

❽ Wenceslas Square

❾ National Museum

❿ Petřín Hill

0 metres 400
0 yards 400

KORUNOVAČNÍ

VELETRŽNÍ

HEŘMANOVA

MILADY HORÁKOVÉ

MILADY

HORÁKOVÉ

LETOHRADSKÁ

KOSTELNÍ

*Letenské sady*
*Letná Park*

Švermův
most

EDVARDA BENEŠE

NÁBŘEŽÍ

Čechův
most

NA FRANTIŠKU

REVOLUČNÍ

NÁBŘEŽÍ LUDVÍKA SVOBODY

BARVÍŘSKÁ

Vltava

17. LISTOPADU

U MILOSRDNÝCH

JOSEFOV
JEWISH
QUARTER

HAŠTALSKÁ

PETRSKÁ

DLOUHÁ

KOZÍ

PAŘÍŽSKÁ

DLOUHÁ

NÁMĚSTÍ JANA
PALACHA

KŘIŽOVNICKÁ

PLATNÉŘSKÁ

KŘIŽOVNICKÉ
NÁMĚSTÍ

MALÉ
NÁMĚSTÍ

STARÉ MĚSTO
OLD TOWN

ANENSKÉ
NÁMĚSTÍ

BETLÉMSKÉ
NÁMĚSTÍ

NA PŘÍKOPĚ

SENOVÁŽNÉ
NÁMĚSTÍ

SMETANOVO NÁBŘEŽÍ

PERLOVÁ

28. ŘÍJNA

JUNGMANNOVO
NÁMĚSTÍ

JINDŘIŠSKÁ

POLITICKÝCH

OPLETALOVA

Vrchlického
Sady

NÁRODNÍ

ŠPÁLENA

OPLETALOVA

VĚZŇ

WASHINGTONOVA

WILSONOVA

NÁBŘEŽÍ

PŠTROSSOVA

NA ZBOŘENCI

ŠPÁLENA

ŠTĚPÁNSKÁ

Čelakovského
Sady

MEZIBRANSKÁ

RUBEŠOVA

ANGLICKÁ

MASARYKOVO

KARLOVO
NÁMĚSTÍ

# PRAGUE CASTLE

**🅒 C2 🄰 Hradčany 🄾 9am–5pm daily 🅦 hrad.cz ↗**

Prague Castle (*Pražský hrad*) is the metaphorical and historical throne of the Czech lands. Around 880 CE, Prince Bořivoj built a wooden fortress on this hilltop, establishing it as the dynastic base of the Přemyslids. In the 14th century the castle became the seat of the Holy Roman Empire. Much of it was rebuilt by Empress Maria Theresa in the 18th century. Today the castle is the official residence of the Czech president.

## 1 Old Royal Palace
While Prince Bořivoj made do with a wooden structure, subsequent residences were built on top of each other as the tastes of Bohemia's rulers changed (*p25*).

## 2 South Gardens
Emperor Ferdinand I gave the castle some greenery in the late 16th century, and First Republic architect Josip Plečnik created the lined paths, steps and grottoes.

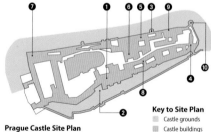

**Prague Castle Site Plan**

**Key to Site Plan**
▫ Castle grounds
▫ Castle buildings

## 3 White Tower
The castle's White Tower was once used as a prison. Today, shops here sell grisly souvenirs. The gangways from which archers once watched over the moat are lined with replicas of weapons.

## 4 Lobkowicz Palace
The only privately owned building in the castle complex, this rival to the National Gallery holds works by Bruegel, Canaletto, Dürer, Rubens and Velázquez.

## 5 St George's Convent
Prince Boleslav II, with Princess Mlada,

Prague Castle looming over the Vltava

still admire the statues of St Peter and St Paul on the façade.

## 8 Rosenberg Palace

This 16th-century palace has had multiple uses: as an 18th-century residence for noble-women, as part of the Ministry of Internal Affairs of Czechoslovakia, and as modern presi-dential offices.

## 9 Golden Lane

In order to avoid paying guild dues in town, goldsmiths lived in these colourful little houses.

## 10 Daliborka Tower

When captured, Dalibor, a Czech Robin Hood figure, became the first prisoner of the tower that now bears his name.

established the first Czech convent for Benedictine nuns here in 973 CE.

## 6 St George's Basilica

Prince Vratislav built the basilica around 920 CE. The 13th-century chapel of St Ludmila is deco-rated with beautiful 16th-century paintings.

## 7 Chapel of the Holy Cross

Built by the Italian architect Anselmo Lurago in 1763, this chapel is usually closed, but you can

*Clockwise from right*
**The ceiling fresco in St George's Basilica; coats of arms on the walls of the Old Royal Palace; colourful houses lining Golden Lane**

**CASTLE GUIDE**

Most of the grounds are free to enter, but tickets to see the interiors are sold at the information centres in the second and third courtyards. Standard tickets include entry to the Old Royal Palace, St George's Basilica, St Vitus Cathedral and Golden Lane (including Daliborka Tower). You can add on the Great South Tower and The Story of Prague Castle *(p25)* exhibition for extra fees.

# Old Royal Palace Features

**Intricate rib vaulting at Vladislav Hall**

## 1. Vladislav Hall
Here, Benedikt Rejt created a mastery of Gothic design with the elaborate vaulting. It has been used for coronations and jousting tournaments, and, since the First Republic, the country's presidents have been ceremoniously sworn in here.

## 2. Louis Wing
Only ten years and a few steps separate the southern wing from the main hall, but in that brief space, Rejt moved castle architecture from Gothic to Renaissance. Bohemian nobles met here in an administrative body when the king was away.

## 3. Bohemian Chancellery
Protestant noblemen threw two Catholic governors and their secretary from the east window, sparking the Thirty Years' War. Their fall was broken by a dung heap – or an intervening angel, depending on who you ask.

## 4. Old Land Rolls Room
The coats of arms on the walls belong to clerks who tracked property ownership and court decisions from 1614 to 1777. Until Maria Theresa, records were unnumbered, identified only by elaborate covers.

## 5. Riders' Staircase
The low steps and vaulted ceiling of this stairway permitted mounted knights to make grand entrances to the spectacular jousting tournaments held in Vladislav Hall.

## 6. Chapel of All Saints
A door leads from Vladislav Hall to a balcony above the Chapel of All Saints, modelled by Petr Parléř on Paris's Gothic Sainte-Chapelle. After fire destroyed it in 1541, it was redesigned in Renaissance style. Of particular artistic note is Hans van Aachen's *Triptych of the Angels*.

## 7. Soběslav Residence
Prince Soběslav built the first stone palace in the 12th century.

## 8. The Story of Prague Castle
This informative and entertaining exhibition covers the history, events, personalities, and arts and crafts relating to the main castle complex.

## 9. Busts from Petr Parléř's Workshop
These impressive effigies, created in the late 14th century, include the grandfather-father-grandson set of John of Luxembourg, Charles IV and Wenceslas IV.

## 10. Diet
Bohemian nobles met the king here in a prototype parliament. The king sat on the throne (the one seen today is a 19th-century replica), the arch-bishop sat on his right, while the estates sat on his left. The portraits on the wall show, from the left, Maria Theresa, her husband Franz, Josef II, Leopold II and Franz I, who fought Napoleon at Austerlitz.

## PRAGUE'S DEFENESTRATIONS

**TOP 10**
RULERS OF PRAGUE

1. Wenceslas
*(around 907–935)*

2. Ottokar II *(1233–78)*

3. Charles IV *(1316–78)*

4. Wenceslas IV
*(1361–1419)*

5. Rudolf II *(1552–1612)*

6. Tomáš Garrigue
Masaryk *(1850–1937)*

7. Edvard Beneš
*(1884–1948)*

8. Gustáv Husák
*(1913–1991)*

9. Václav Havel
*(1936–2011)*

10. Petr Pavel *(b 1961)*

Prague's first recorded instance of execution by hurling the condemned people from a window occurred at the outset of the Hussite Wars in 1419. Vladislav II's officials met a similar fate in 1483. Perhaps as a tribute to their forebears, more than 100 Protestant nobles stormed the Old Royal Palace in 1618 and cast two hated Catholic governors and their secretary out of the window. Protestants said the men's fall was broken by a dung heap swept from the Vladislav Hall after a recent tournament, while Catholics claimed they were saved by angels. The incident is often cited as the spark that began the Thirty Years' War. After the defeat of the Protestants by the army of the Holy Roman Emperor Ferdinand II at the first skirmish at White Mountain *(p30)*, 27 of these nobles were executed in the Old Town Square *(p28)*.

**Clash between Protestant and Catholic forces at White Mountain**

# ST VITUS CATHEDRAL

📍 C2 🏛 Third Courtyard, Prague Castle 🕐 Apr–Oct: 9am–5pm Mon–Sat, noon–5pm Sun; Nov–Mar: 9am–4pm daily 🌐 katedralasvatehovita.cz 🔗

The spectacular Gothic *Katedrála svatého Víta* is an unmissable sight in Prague, not least because of its dominant position on Hradčany hill. Prince Wenceslas first built a rotunda here on a pagan worship site and dedicated it to St Vitus (*svatý Vít*), a Roman saint.

**The soaring Great South Tower**

is clear. When work resumed after the war, architectural preferences had moved towards the Renaissance, hence the rounded cap that can be seen on a Gothic base.

**TOP TIP**

The Royal Crypt can only be accessed through a guided tour.

## 1 Great South Tower

The point at which the Hussite Wars halted construction of this 96-m (315-ft) tower

## 2 Royal Crypt

The greatest kings of Bohemia are buried in a single room beneath the cathedral, including Charles IV, Wenceslas IV and Rudolf II.

## 3 High Altar

Bounded by St Vitus Chapel and the marble sarcophagi of Ferdinand I and

family, the high altar and chancel follow Neo-Gothic philosophy.

## 4 Golden Portal

This triple-arched arcade was the main cathedral entrance until the western end was completed in the 20th century. It is still used on special occasions.

St Wenceslas's tomb, Wenceslas Chapel

## 5 Bohemian Crown Jewels

You'd think there would be a safer place for the crown and sceptre of Bohemia, but the coronation chamber of Wenceslas Chapel is said to be guarded by the spirit of the saint.

## 6 The Tomb of St John of Nepomuk

The silver for this 1,680-kg (3,700-lb) coffin came from the Bohemian mining town Kutná Hora, signified by the miners' statues to the left of the tomb.

## 7 New Archbishop's Chapel

Czech artists Alfons Mucha created the Art Nouveau window

Neo-Gothic interior of the cathedral

of the Slavic saints for the chapel. Despite appearances, the glass is painted, not stained.

## 8 Sigismund

One of four Renaissance bells in the Great South Tower, the 18-tonne bell (20 ton) known as Sigismund is the nation's largest and dates from 1549. It takes four volunteers to ring the bell on important church holidays and at events.

## 9 Royal Oratory

The royals crossed a narrow bridge from the Old Royal Palace (p22) to this private gallery for Mass. The coats of arms represent all the countries ruled by Vladislav II.

## 10 Wenceslas Chapel

This stands on the site of the first rotunda and

contains St Wenceslas's tomb. The frescoes of Christ's Passion on the lower wall are surrounded by 1,300 semi-precious stones. To celebrate his son Ludvik's coronation, Vladislav II commissioned the upper frescoes of St Wenceslas's life.

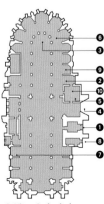

St Vitus Cathedral Floorplan

# OLD TOWN SQUARE

📍 M3 🏠 Staré Město

As the heart and soul of the city, the Old Town Square (*Staroměstské náměstí*) is hard to miss. There was a marketplace here in the 11th century, but it was in 1338, when John of Luxembourg gave Prague's burghers permission to form a town council, that the Old Town Hall was built and the square came into its own. Today, it has a lively atmosphere, with café tables set out in front of painted façades.

**1 Dům u Minuty**
The "House at the Minute" probably takes its name from the not-so-minute *sgraffito* images on its walls. The alchemical symbols adorning Staroměstské náměstí 2 date from 1610. Writer Franz Kafka (*p56*) lived in the black-and-white house as a boy, from 1889 to 1896.

**2 House at the Stone Bell**
Formerly done up in Baroque style, workers discovered the Gothic façade of this house as late as 1980. On the southwestern corner is the bell which gives the house its name. The Municipal Gallery often hosts temporary exhibitions here.

**3 Church of Our Lady before Týn**
This Gothic edifice began as a humble church (*p51*) serving residents in the

Stunning *sgraffito* on Dům u Minuty

**Prague's famous
Old Town Square**

### 5 Jan Hus Memorial
Hus was burned at the stake in 1415 for proposing radical church reform. The inscription below his figure at the 1915 memorial reads "Truth Will Prevail".

### 6 Marian Column
On Czechoslovakia's declaration of independence in 1918, this former column reminded jubilant mobs of Habsburg rule and they tore it down. In 2020, the column was reconstructed.

### 7 Ungelt
The courtyard behind Týn church was home to foreign merchants in the 14th century, but today it houses smart boutiques and cafés.

### 8 Kinský Palace
This Rococo palace, found at Staroměstské náměstí 12, now houses the National Gallery's temporary exhibitions (p122). It was once home to the haberdashery owned by Franz Kafka's father, Hermann.

### 9 Malé náměstí
The ornate well in the centre of the "Small Square" doubles as a plague memorial. The elaborate murals of crafters on the façade of Rott House were designed by Mikoláš Aleš. From the 19th century to the early 1990s, the building was an ironmongery.

### 10 Štorch House
At Staroměstské náměstí 16, the focal points are Art Nouveau paintings of St Wenceslas (the patron saint of Bohemia) and the three Magi.

> **JAN HUS**
>
> The rector of Prague University, Jan Hus was dedicated to fighting against corruption in the church. Declared a heretic by the church, he was burned at the stake. Czech resentment turned into civil war, with Hussite rebels facing the power of Rome. But the Hussites split into moderate and radical factions. Hus is still a national figure – 6 July, the day he was killed, is a public holiday.

> **EAT**
> Take a break from the sites at the historic Restaurace Mincovna found in the corner of the square (restaurace mincovna.cz).

mercantile town (týn) in the 14th century. Following architectural customs of the time, the south tower is stouter than the north one; they are said to depict Adam and Eve.

### 4 St Nicholas Cathedral
Prague has two Baroque churches of St Nicholas, both built by Kilian Ignac Dientzenhofer. The architect completed the one, called the cathedral now, in Staré Město two years before starting Malá Strana's (p96). Regular concerts here are worth a visit.

**Jan Hus Memorial in Old Town Square**

# Old Town Hall Features

### 1. Astronomical Clock
During the day, bells ring, cocks crow and 15th-century statues dance on the hour while crowds of tourists watch from below.

### 2. Apostles
Marionette artist Vojtěch Sucharda carved the 12 wooden figures that emerge from the clock every hour – they replace the ones destroyed by German artillery in 1945.

### 3. Municipal Hall
This was once the central point of the building where all the most important matters concerning the administration of Prague's Staré Město were discussed.

### 4. Dukla Memorial
Behind a brass plaque marked with the year 1944 is a pot of soil from the Dukla battlefield. German artillery killed and wounded around 70,000 Red Army soldiers in this Slovak pass in one of the most grievous Soviet miscalculations of World War II.

### 5. White Mountain Memorial
In the pavement on the town hall's eastern side are set 27 crosses in memory of the Bohemian nobles who were executed for their role in the Thirty Years' War. After the Battle of White Mountain (p9), the men were publicly hanged, beheaded or drawn and quartered here.

### 6. Gothic Chapel
The small chapel adjoining the Mayors' Hall was consecrated in 1381 in honour of Sts Wenceslas, Vitus and Ludmila. Wenceslas IV's emblem and his wife Eufemia's initial adorn the entrance portal. In the nave is a model of the Marian column (p29) which stood on the square until 1918 and was returned in 2020.

**Spiral staircase leading to the Astronomical Clock**

### 7. Elevator
The elevator to the viewing gallery of the tower won a design award in 1999. Oddly enough, its space-age design works harmoniously with the stony surroundings. It also permits wheelchair access to the top of the tower – a rare consideration in Prague.

### 8. Viewing Gallery
The parapet under the Old Town Hall's roof affords visitors a unique view of the square and Staré Město below. A little pocket change will buy you two minutes on a miniature telescope, with which you can admire the Prague Valley.

### 9. Gothic Cellars
The cellars of the Old Town Hall were once ground-floor rooms. The town was subject to flooding, so more earth was added to keep the burghers' feet dry. The spaces were used as granaries as well as debtors' prisons.

### 10. The Green
The Old Town Hall's north wing was severely damaged in an urban fight between the Germans and the Czechs during World War II. After the war, the wing was torn down. Now there is a quiet area with benches to sit and escape the crowds.

**TOP 10**
FEATURES OF THE
ASTRONOMICAL CLOCK

1. Solar clock
2. Lunar clock
3. Josef Mánes Calendar
4. Apostles
5. Angel and the Sciences
6. Vanity, Avarice, Death and Lust
7. Rooster
8. Hourly shows
9. Mikuláš of Kadaň
10. Dial

## BUILDING THE OLD TOWN HALL

Prague's Staré Město received its charter and fortifications from John of Luxembourg in 1338, but its town clerk had to wait nearly 150 years for an office. The Old Town Hall was cobbled together from existing houses over the centuries until it comprised the five houses that stand at Staroměstské náměstí 1–2 today. The town hall's eastern wing once stretched to within a few feet of St Nicholas Cathedral *(p91)*, but in 1945 German artillery bombardment reduced it to rubble. The 69.5-m (228-ft) tower was built in 1364, and in 1410 the imperial clockmaker Mikuláš of Kadaň created the basic mechanism of the Prague Orloj, or Astronomical Clock. In 1552 Jan Táborský was put in charge, and by 1566 the clock was fully mechanized.

**The Astronomical Clock on the Old Town Hall**

# CHARLES BRIDGE

📍 J4 📍 Karlův Most

The spectacular Charles Bridge *(Karlův most)* has witnessed battles, executions and, increasingly, film shoots. Architect Petr Parléř built it in Gothic style to replace its predecessor, the Judith Bridge. The bridge's most distinguishing feature is its gallery of 30 statues. The religious figures were installed from 1683 onwards to lead people back to the church. Today all the statues are copies, with the originals in museums.

**1 Calvary**
This statue will cause double-takes among students of Hebrew. According to a nearby apologia, the words "Holy, holy, holy is the Lord of Hosts" were added in 1696, paid for by a local Jewish man who had been accused of profaning the cross.

**2 Old Town Bridge Tower**
This beautiful Gothic tower, designed by Petr Parléř *(p27)*, was built at the end of the 14th century. Visitors can climb the 138 stairs to the viewing gallery for a jaw-dropping panoramic view of the city.

**3 The Lorraine Cross**
Midway across the bridge is a brass cross where St John of Nepomuk's body was thrown into the river. It is said that wishes made at the cross will come true.

**4 Statue of St John of Nepomuk**
At the base of the statue of St John is a brass relief showing a man diving into the river. Rubbing it to attract good luck is an old local tradition; petting the adjacent brass dog is a new one.

**5 Statue of Sts Cyril and Methodius**
Greek missionaries who brought both Christianity and the Glagolitic alphabet to the Czech and Slovak lands, Cyril and Methodius are revered figures in both countries to this day.

**6 Statue of Bruncvik**
Peer over the bridge's southern edge to see the Czech answer to King Arthur. Bruncvik, a mythical Bohemian knight, is said to have had a magical sword and helped a lion fight

*Clockwise from right*
**Calvary sculpture featuring the crucifix; statue of St John of Nepomuk; bronze relief depicting the martyrdom of St John of Nepomuk**

a seven-headed dragon. He and his army are promised to awaken and save Prague at the city's most desperate hour.

## 7 Our Lady of the Mangles

The portrait of Mary hanging on the house south of the bridge is tied to an ancient tale of miraculous healing. Seeing the light go out on the balcony below is supposedly an omen of imminent death – don't stare too long.

## 8 Statue of St Luitgard

Matthias Braun's 1710 depiction of a blind Cistercian nun's celebrated vision, in which Christ appeared to her and permitted her to touch his wounds, has a timeless appeal.

## 9 Malá Strana Bridge Towers

Charles Bridge ends at the stone archway connecting Malá Strana's two bridge towers. The smaller, stockier structure on the left is the Judith Tower, which dates to the 12th century.

**Historic Charles Bridge at sunrise**

## 10 Statue of the Trinitarian Order

This religious order was set up to ransom prisoners of war from the Crusades and buy Christians back their freedom.

### WHEN TO VISIT CHARLES BRIDGE

During summer, and increasingly year-round, the bridge is well nigh impassable throughout the day, crowded with artists and tourists. It is best seen in the early hours as the sun rises over the Old Town bridge tower. A late evening stroll gives a similarly dramatic view, with the illuminated cathedral and castle looming above.

# LORETA

📍 B2 🏠 Loretánské náměstí 7 🕐 10am–5pm daily 🌐 loreta.cz ♿

At the heart of this sparkling 17th-century Baroque pilgrimage site is its claim to fame and most proud possession: a replica of the original Santa Casa in Loreto, Italy, believed to be the house where the Virgin Mary received the Incarnation. Construction of the church and the surrounding chapels coincided with the Counter-Reformation, and was intended to lure Czechs back to the Catholic faith.

**1 Loretánské náměstí**

This historic square is said to have originally been a pagan burial ground. The elegant stucco façade of Loreta is dwarfed by the Černín Palace opposite, home of the Ministry of Foreign Affairs.

**2 Santa Casa**

The beautiful stucco reliefs on the exterior of this replica of the Holy Family's house in Nazareth depict scenes from the life of the Virgin Mary. Inside stands the miracle-working statue of Our Lady of Loreto.

**3 Bell Tower**

The carillon was the gift of a merchant of Prague whose daughter was healed by the intercession of the Lady of Loreto.

**4 Inner Courtyard**

In this courtyard, visitors can admire two Baroque fountains. The south fountain depicts the Assumption of the Virgin; the north

**Exquisite ceiling frescoes in the church**

**Loreta Floorplan**

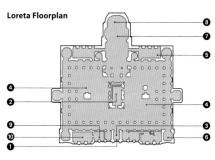

**Loreta's Baroque church complex** features a sculpture of the Resurrection.

**5 Arcade**
Before and after visiting the Santa Casa, pilgrims passed through the arcade and prayed at its chapels dedicated to the Holy Family, the Holy Rood, St Francis Seraphim, St Antony of Padua, St Anne and Our Lady of Sorrows.

**6 St Wilgefortis Altar**
The Chapel of Our Lady of Sorrows contains the altar of a bearded, cruci-fied woman. Wilgefortis was said to be a maiden who prayed for a mascu-line appearance in order to preserve her chastity.

**7 Church of the Nativity**
Originally a small alcove behind the Santa Casa,

the church was expanded into its present size in 1717. The Rococo organ stands opposite the altar, over a crypt to Loreta benefactors.

**8 Altars of Sts Felicissimus and Marcia**
On either side of the altar in the Church of the Nativity are large reliquary displays con-taining the remains of these two Spanish saints.

**9 Prague Sun**
The silver monstrance for displaying the host – created in 1699 by Johann Bernard Fischer von Erlach – is gold-plated and studded with 6,222 diamonds.

**Diamond-encrusted Prague Sun**

The Virgin looks up at her son, represented by the host in the receptacle.

**10 Treasury**
The Communists created this exhibit of sacred items to show how the papal church brought peasants to obedience with a "cheap promise of happiness beyond the grave".

**SANTA CASA**

The Santa Casa was the house in Nazareth in which the archangel Gabriel is believed to have announced to the Virgin Mary that she would conceive the Son of God. In the 13th century, the Greek Angeli family moved the house to Loreto, Italy. Copies of the Italian Loreto started emerging all over Europe – the 17th-century Prague site is believed to be the truest representation of the original structure.

# THE JEWISH MUSEUM

☒ jewishmuseum.cz ☒

Prague's magnificent Jewish Museum encompasses not just one building but many: four synagogues, the Old Jewish Cemetery, Ceremonial Hall and Robert Guttmann Gallery. Admission to all sites is covered by a single ticket, available from the Visitor Centre or online. Though not formally part of the museum, admission includes the Old-New Synagogue, Europe's oldest surviving synagogue.

## 1 Visitor Centre

⌂ Maiselova 38/15
🕐 Nov–Mar: Hours vary, chech website

Start your visit at the Visitor Centre, where you will find information on each of the museum's sites along with ticket and reservation options.

## 2 Klausen Synagogue

The museum's largest synagogue (p114) was built in grand Baroque style in 1694 and houses exhibitions that focus on Jewish traditions and culture, which includes family rituals connected to birth, circumcision and marriage. The synagogue is currently undergoing reconstruction work but will reopen in 2025.

## 3 Pinkas Synagogue

Originally a private prayer house, this 15th-century Gothic structure (p114) is today home to the highly moving "Wall of Commemoration" and an equally emotional exhibition showcasing drawings created by children held at the Nazi-run Terezín (Theresienstadt) ghetto during World War II.

## 4 Wall of Commemoration

Located within the Pinkas Synagogue (p114), this memorial wall is a beautiful tribute to an estimated 80,000 Czech and Moravians victims of the Holocaust, whose remains could not be returned for burial.

### ROBERT GUTTMANN

Prague painter Robert Guttmann (1880–1942) was as much known for his art as for his eccentric appearance and ambitious treks on foot around Europe. In October 1941, the Nazis transported Guttman on the first bus to the Jewish ghetto in Łódź, Poland, where he died six months later.

## 5 Robert Guttmann Gallery

Named for painter Robert Guttmann, this gallery hosts a collection of works by Guttman along with temporary exhibitions on Jewish history and culture. Be sure to consult the museum website to see what's on.

## 6 Ceremonial Hall

The ornate Ceremonial Hall (p114) was once the home of Prague's Burial Society, a religious

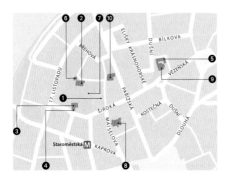

Stunning Moorish interior of the Spanish Synagogue

institution in the ghetto, and many of the rooms were used for parts of the funeral process. Today, it houses an exhibition that covers the society and features artifacts that include ritual objects and memorial prayers.

### 7 Old Jewish Cemetery

The crumbling Old Jewish Cemetery *(Starý židovský hřbitov)* was one of the few burial sites available to Prague's Jews. Space was so limited that graves had to be layered when the plot was full. Around 12,000 headstones are visible, dating from 1439 to 1787, with hundreds of thousands buried below.

### 8 Maisel Synagogue

The private synagogue *(p114)* of the 16th-century mayor of the Jewish Quarter and wealthy benefactor, Mordechai Maisel, today it has a permanent exhibition on Jewish history in the Czech Republic from the 10th to 18th centuries.

### 9 Spanish Synagogue

Richly decorated inside and out, this Moorish style synagogue from the mid-19th century is the most recent addition to the Jewish Quarter. The synagogue *(p113)* houses a continuation of the Maisel Synagogue's exhibition, with the story of local Jewish life in the 19th and 20th centuries.

### 10 Old-New Synagogue

This evocative synagogue *(p114)* is one of the city's oldest Gothic structures and is still a working synagogue today. Among the highlights are Rabbi Loew's chair; 12 windows of the nave, which evoke the 12 tribes of Israel; and the ark housing sacred Torah scrolls.

Outside the Old-New Synagogue

# Old Jewish Cemetery

**1. Avigdor Kara's Grave**
The oldest grave is that of this poet and scholar, known for his documentation of the pogrom of 1389, which he survived.

**2. Mordechai Maisel's Grave**
Mordechai Maisel (1528–1601), the mayor of the Jewish ghetto during the reign of Rudolf II, funded the synagogue (p114) that bears his name.

**3. Klausen Synagogue**
Mordechai Maisel also commissioned the building of the Klausen Synagogue (p114) on the cemetery's northern edge. It now houses exhibitions (p36) on Jewish festivals and traditions.

**4. Gothic Tombstones**
The eastern wall has fragments of Gothic tombstones rescued from another graveyard near Vladislavova street in 1866. Further graves at another site were found in the 1990s.

**5. Hendl Bassevi's Grave**
This elaborate tombstone (below) marks the resting place of the "Jewish Queen", Hendl Bassevi. Her husband, mayor Jacob Bassevi, was raised to the nobility by Ferdinand II and permitted a coat of arms, which can be seen on his wife's gravestone.

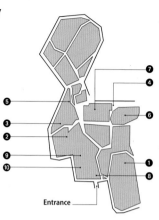

**Old Jewish Cemetery Site Map**

**Tombstone of Hendl Bassevi**

**6. Nephele Mound**
Stillborn children, miscarried babies and other infants who died under a year old were buried in the southeast corner of the cemetery.

**7. Grave of Rabbi Judah Loew**
The grave of Rabbi Judah Loew ben Bezalel (p114), to whom legend attributes the creation of the Prague Golem (p60), is located here.

**8. David Gans's Tombstone**
Gans's headstone is marked with a goose and the Star of David, after his name and his faith. A pupil of Loew, Gans (1541–1613) was the author of a two-volume history of the Jewish people and an accomplished astronomer during the time of Johannes Kepler.

**9. Grave of Rabbi Oppenheim**
Rabbi David Oppenheim was the first chief rabbi of Moravia, and later chief rabbi of Bohemia and finally of Prague, where he died in 1736.

**10. Zemach Grave**
The gravestone of the printer Mordechai Zemach (d 1592) and his son Bezalel (d 1589) lies next to the Pinkas Synagogue (p114). Mordechai Zemach was a co-founder of the Prague Burial Society.

**TOP 10**
JEWISH LEADERS

1. Eliezer ben Elijah Ashkenazi (1512–85)

2. Judah Loew ben Bezalel (c 1520–1609)

3. Mordechai Maisel (1528–1601)

4. Mordechai ben Abraham Jaffe (1530–1612)

5. Ephraim Solomon ben Aaron of Luntshits (1550–1619)

6. Joseph Solomon Delmedigo (1591–1655)

7. David ben Abraham Oppenheim (1664–1736)

8. Yechezkel ben Yehuda Landau (1713–93)

9. Solomon Judah Lieb Rapoport (1790–1867)

10. Efraim Karol Sidon (b 1942)

## PRAGUE'S JEWISH COMMUNITY

Prague's Jewish community has been integral to the development of the city. Prominent Jewish people, like Rabbi Loew (p114) and Mordechai Maisel paved the way for Jewish participation in the National Revival of the 19th century. In the 20th century, the works of Jewish author Franz Kafka (p56) reached global fame – today, the Kafka Museum is one of the city's biggest draws. However, since arriving in the 10th century, Prague's Jewish community has been continuously subject to anti-Semitism. Pogroms such as the infamous Passover slaughter of 1389 – in which 3,000 Jewish people were killed – have devastated the community. Violence has persisted over the centuries. Notably, the 1899 trial of Leopold Hilsner (a Jewish man accused of ritual murder) began an anti-Jewish campaign in the city. Support for Hilsner from Tomáš Garrigue Masaryk, future President of Czechoslovakia, helped sway public opinion to some degree. In 1939, after the Nazis occupied Prague, the Jewish population was systematically deported to concentration camps. By the end of the war, nearly 80,000 Jewish people from Bohemia and Moravia had died in the Holocaust; Prague's Jewish population has never fully recovered.

**Former Jewish ghetto of Staré Město in the early 20th century**

# 7

# ST AGNES OF BOHEMIA CONVENT

📍 M1 📍 U Milosrdných 17 🕐 10am–6pm Tue–Sun 🌐 ngprague.cz ↗

The 13th-century St Agnes of Bohemia Convent (*Klášter sv. nežky Ceské*) is a Gothic building closely tied to Czech statehood. Daughter of Czech King Přemyšl Ottokar I, Princess Agnes founded a convent here in 1234 for the Poor Clares, an order of nuns associated with the Order of St Francis. Restored in the 1980s, the convent is now part of the National Gallery and exhibits medieval and early Renaissance art.

## 1 Strakonice Madonna

This larger-than-life, 700-year-old statue of the Virgin and Child is the Czech National Gallery's most prized possession. The gestures of the Madonna are strikingly rigid, and evoke the Classical French sculpture found in places such as Reims Cathedral.

## 2 Zbraslav Madonna

Bohemia's most celebrated Marian painting is evocative of Byzantine icons in its style. The ring on the Madonna's left-hand finger symbolizes the church through the mystical marriage between Christ and the Virgin Mary. The work was moved to the St Agnes of Bohemia Convent from the Cistercian Zbraslav Monastery where the majority of the Přemyslid kings were laid to rest.

## 3 Vyšší Brod Altarpiece

The 14th-century cycle begins with the Annunciation, then proceeds through the

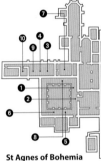

**St Agnes of Bohemia Convent Floorplan**

Adoration of the Magi to Pentecost. The creator of these beautiful panels is unknown.

*Clockwise from below right*
**Gothic exterior of the convent; the 14th-century *Zbraslav Madonna* painting; Velhartice altarpiece**

## 4 Works of Master Theodoricus

Parts of an altar set on loan from Karlštejn Castle, these works include *St Charlemagne, St Catherine, St Matthew, St Luke, St Ambrose* and *St Gregory*.

## 5 Puchner Altarpiece

St Agnes gave up a life at court to pursue a spiritual vocation. On this 15th-century altarpiece, she is typically depicted nursing the sick.

## 6 Třeboň Altarpiece

Only three of the five panels of the 14th-century retable Třebon Altarpiece

**Medieval art from the National Gallery**

have survived to the present day.

## 7 Capuchin Cycle

The origin of these fascinating 14 painted panels is unknown. The Virgin Mary is flanked by St Peter on the left and Christ on the right

## 8 Velhartice Altarpiece

Originating in south Bohemia around 1500, this is a rare example of a completely preserved altar.

## 9 Martyrdom of St Florian

Albrecht Altdorfer created this painting as part of a multipanel altar featuring scenes from the legend of St Florian. Other pieces from the series are in Florence.

## 10 Apocalypse Cycle

Although Albrecht Dürer is considered the foremost German Renaissance artist, he is known to many for his woodcuts, which date from 1498 and retain a strong Gothic flavour.

### ST AGNES OF BOHEMIA

St Agnes of Bohemia was a powerful figure in medieval politics. Gregory IX granted her convent special privileges. Agnes died in 1282, but her influence on Czech statehood was felt in 1989, when Pope John Paul II canonized her; five days later, the Velvet Revolution (p11) began.

# 8

# WENCESLAS SQUARE

📍 N6 🏠 Nové Město

This former medieval horse market began to be redeveloped in the 19th century, rapidly becoming the commercial hub of Prague. In 1848 it was renamed Wenceslas Square (*Václavské náměstí*) in honour of Bohemia's patron saint. The majority of the buildings seen today date from the early 20th century, and have beautiful Art Nouveau façades.

### 1 National Museum

Invading Warsaw Pact troops shelled the Neo-Renaissance building (p44) in 1968, mistaking it for the country's parliament. The entry fee is worth it, if only to see the grand marble stairway and pantheon of Czech cultural figures.

### 2 St Wenceslas Statue

The Přemyslid prince sits astride a horse flanked by other Czech patrons in Josef Myslbek's 1912 sculpture. The area "under the tail" is a traditional meeting place for locals.

### 3 Communist Memorial

In front of St Wenceslas is a memorial to the victims of Communism, such as the two men who

>  **EAT**
> There are cafés, restaurants and shops lined up on both sides of Wenceslas Square from top to bottom. Visit any of these for a delicious meal.

**Imposing National Museum building**

**Prague's bustling Wenceslas Square**

### 6 Grand Hotel Evropa

Built between 1903 and 1906, this Art Nouveau building is an architectural gem. The interior is closed for renovation, but its beautifully preserved façade can still be seen.

**Mosaic, Church of Our Lady of the Snows**

### 7 Upside-Down Statue

Hanging in the central passage of the Palác Lucerna is David Černý's take *(p68)* on Czech patron saint Wenceslas.

### 8 Franciscan Garden

A stone's throw from the busy Wenceslas Square, this former monastery garden *(p119)* provides much-needed peace from the city bustle.

### 9 Church of Our Lady of the Snows

Founded by Charles IV upon his coronation

died protesting against the 1968 invasion.

### 4 Palác Koruna

Built in 1912 in Geometric Modernist style, this "palace" held offices, homes and Turkish-style baths. The listed building now hosts the Koruna Palace shopping centre, which has several cafés and luxury stores.

### 5 Palác Lucerna

Václav Havel's grandfather designed and built this building, now home to an art gallery, cinema, cafés, shops and a ballroom.

in 1347, this beautiful church was supposed to have been more than 100 m (330 ft) long, but it was never completed.

### 10 Crisis Fallout Shelter

Hidden under the Hotel Jalta, on the square, is a nuclear bunker, built in 1953 for high-ranking officials in the so-called "Stalin's Baroque" style. It is now part of the Cold War Museum (en.muzeum -studene-valky.cz).

**HISTORIC DEMONSTRATIONS**

Wenceslas Square saw its first demonstration in 1419 when Catholic reformer Jan Želivský led a procession to St Stephen's Church. On 28 October 1918 the area witnessed Czechoslovak independence. In 1969, student Jan Palach set himself on fire here as a political protest against the Soviet occupation.

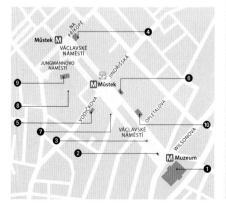

# 9

# NATIONAL MUSEUM

📍 G5 🏛 Václavské náměstí 68 🕙 10am–6pm daily 🌐 nm.cz 📷📱

The National Museum (*Národní museum*) is one of the city's most remarkable buildings and a glimmering repository of cultural and natural artifacts. The museum was conceived in the 19th century as a grand expression of Czech national identity. These days, the museum is housed in two separate buildings linked by a tunnel, and features the country's preeminent collections of natural and ethnographic history.

Exhibition of various minerals

## 1 Entrance Hall

You can't fail to notice the Neo-Renaissance interiors of the stunning entrance. The highlight is the grand stairway, but you'll find marble pillars, elaborate frescoes and a shimmering glass ceiling with dizzying views up to the cupola.

## 2 History Exhibition

Seven halls on the main building's first floor are devoted to this sprawling display of historical artifacts, which recounts major historical events from the early medieval period (8th century) to the start of World War I.

## 3 Halls of Minerals

The first floor is home to a grand exhibition of 4,000 minerals as well as impactites, meteorites and tektites (glass-like debris formed during a meteorite impact). A great place for budding geologists to geek out.

## 4 Windows into Prehistory

Fossils and models of prehistoric animals are spread out over four rooms on the first floor. Look out for an eye-popping model of the Czech Republic's only native dinosaur, the Burianosaurus.

## 5 Pantheon

Magnificent intricate busts of famous Czech scholars, writers and artists stand below the cupola on the main building's second floor.

## 6 Miracles of Evolution

The long story of evolution is recounted through lively exhibits on the second floor of the

main building, stuffed with life-sized models of creatures from the animal kingdom, including a white shark and a 17-m- (55-ft-) long giant squid.

## 7 Cupola (Dome)

Unafraid of heights? Ride the lift up to the soaring dome for magical views over the city. In the

Ornate interior of the museum

**TOP TIP**

On the first Monday of every month, entry to both sites of the museum is free.

distance, you can see the spires of Prague Castle.

## 8 Moments of History

Descend to the underground corridor that links the main building with its annex. An innovative multimedia exhibition projected on the walls traces the history of the city from pre-history to the present.

## 9 Children's Museum

The museum is a haven for curious young minds. Occupying the second floor of the annex are three halls filled with interactive games and exhibits that can teach little ones about subjects from natural selection to Prague's role in WWII.

## 10 History of the 20th Century

A bewildering multimedia exhibition on the annex's fourth floor continues Prague's story, from the start of World War I through to the collapse of communism in 1989 and beyond.

**BULLET HOLES**

The main building is so illustrious that invading Soviet troops in August 1968 mistook it for Czechoslovakia's parliament and riddled the front exterior with bullets, which remained visible despite Communist attempts to cover them up. The building was renovated in the 2010s, but if you look closely, you can still see faint imprints where the bullets struck the façade.

# 10

# PETŘÍN HILL

⊙ B4  ⌂ Malá Strana

**Covered with forests and orchards, Petřín Hill is a soft counterpoint to the spires of Hradčany on the Vltava's left bank. Rising more than 300 m (1,000 ft) above sea level, the area began life as a vineyard in the 15th century, but has been a public park since 1825. This park is the perfect place to take a break from the city – stroll along old pathways or take the funicular to see the sights atop the hill.**

## 1 Observation Tower

Modelled after the Eiffel Tower in Paris, Petřín Hill's 63.5-m (210-ft) Eiffelovka stands only one-quarter as high as its inspiration. The tower was created for the Jubilee Exposition of 1891. A climb of 299 stairs leads to the viewing platform.

## 2 Strahov Stadium

This stadium is the largest arena of its kind in the world. Built for Sokol, a physical exercise organization, it was used for gymnastic rallies. Today it is a rock concert venue.

**EAT**
Nebozízek restaurant, situated right in the middle of Petřín Park, offers delicious food along with spectacular views of Petřín Hill and its surroundings.

Onion-domed towers, Church of St Lawrence

### 3 Strahov Monastery

Founded in 1140, Strahov houses the nation's oldest books in the Strahov Library while still functioning as a monastery. The Theological Hall, with its frescoes and statue of St John, is a must-see.

### 4 Hunger Wall

The 14th-century wall was once part of the city's southern fortifications. Charles IV is said to have ordered its construction as a project to feed the poor during a famine.

### 5 Mirror Maze

After laughing at the distorting mirrors in the labyrinth (p71), take in a bit of history with a diorama depicting the last major military action of the Thirty Years' War on Charles Bridge. On the roof of the maze, there are weather vanes with the

Observation Tower on Petřín Hill

names of the workers who worked on the construction in 1891.

### 6 Church of St Lawrence

This onion-domed church was built on a pagan shrine in the 10th century and rebuilt in Baroque style in the 18th century.

### 7 Karel Hynek Mácha Statue

Mácha is a national poet, best loved for his Romantic poem "May". On 1 May, admirers lay flowers at his statue.

### 8 Štefánik's Observatory

Operating since 1928, the observatory was named after M R Štefánik, a Slovak diplomat, scientist and astronomer and the co founder of the Czechoslovak Republic.

### 9 Kinský Summer Palace

On the Smíchov side of Petřín Hill, this 19th-century palace

STRAHOV MONASTERY EXHIBITS

Strahov has suffered pillaging armies, fires and totalitarian regimes. Josef II dissolved most local monasteries in 1783, sparing Strahov on the condition that the monks conduct research at their library. Today the majority of the research involves paper preservation. On display are old books, pictures, ornate gospels and miniature Bibles.

houses the National Museum's ethno-graphic collections.

### 10 Funicular

Do as visitors have done since 1890 and take the funicular railway to the top of the hill and walk down. The cable car offers outstanding views of the castle to the north.

Funicular heading to the top of the hill

# TOP 10 OF EVERYTHING

| | |
|---|---|
| Churches | 50 |
| Historical Sites | 52 |
| Museums and Galleries | 54 |
| Writers and Composers | 56 |
| House Signs | 58 |
| Myths and Legends | 60 |
| Eccentric Prague | 64 |
| Parks and Gardens | 66 |
| Off the Beaten Track | 68 |
| Family Attractions | 70 |
| Performing Arts Venues | 72 |
| Nights Out | 74 |
| Prague Dishes | 76 |
| Bars and Kavárnas | 78 |
| Shops and Markets | 80 |
| Prague for Free | 82 |
| Festivals | 84 |

*Handpainted Easter eggs*

# PLACES OF WORSHIP

## 1 Loreta

At the heart of this elaborate shrine to the Virgin Mary is the Santa Casa – a reproduction of the house where Mary received the Angel Gabriel. Loreta's treasury (p35) holds several priceless monstrances and other artifacts.

## 2 St Vitus Cathedral

The current building, looming majestically over the castle complex, is a combination of architectural styles and took almost 600 years to complete. In days of old, the cathedral (p26) was the setting for spectacular Bohemian coronations conducted by Prague's archbishops. It is also the final resting place of the saints John of Nepomuk and Wenceslas, as well as scores of other notable Czech figures.

Colourful stained glass,
St Vitus Cathedral

## 3 Old-New Synagogue

Prague's Orthodox Jewish community (p39) still holds services in this 13th-century synagogue (p114), which is the oldest in Central Europe. Its curious name may come from the Hebrew Al-Tenai, meaning "with reservation". Legend has it that its stones will eventually have to be returned to Jerusalem, whence they came.

## 4 St Nicholas Church, Malá Strana

The Malá Strana church clock tower and dome upstage its namesake across the river. The splendid Baroque sanctuary (p98) was meant to impress Catholic sceptics of the might of Rome.

## 5 Church of our Lady Victorious

This Baroque church contains the famed statue (p99) of the Infant Jesus of Prague. The wax baby doll is credited with miraculous powers. The resident Order of English Virgins looks after the statue and changes his clothes.

## 6 Basilica of St James

This is an active place of worship. The Baroque façade (p90) is awash with cherubs and scenes depicting episodes from the lives of saints

**Striking Basilica of St James soaring over Prague**

Francis of Assisi, James and Antony of Padua. There is also a mummified arm hanging above the door inside.

# 7 Church of Our Lady before Týn

🚇 M3 🏛 Staroměstské náměstí 14 🕐 10am–1pm & 3–5pm Tue–Sat, 10:30am–noon Sun

The Gothic towers of Týn loom over Old Town Square's houses. During the Counter-Reformation, the Jesuits melted down the gold Hussite chalice that stood between the towers and recast it as the Madonna seen today.

# 8 Pinkas Synagogue

The names of nearly 80,000 Czech victims of the Holocaust (p36) cover the walls of this notable house (p114), which sits adjacent to the Old Jewish Cemetery. The women's gallery was added in the 18th century.

# 9 Cathedral of Sts Cyril and Methodius

The assassins of Reinhard Heydrich, the Nazi governor of Czechoslovakia, took refuge in this Eastern Orthodox cathedral (p119) along with members of the Czech Resistance. Surrounded by German troops, they took their own lives on 18 June 1942. The Nazis executed Bishop Gorazd, who had sheltered them.

# 10 Spanish Synagogue

The present Moorish building with its opulent interior (p113) replaced Prague's oldest synagogue after the latter was razed in 1867. The Conservative Jewish community holds services here. It also houses Jewish Museum exhibits, offices and a reference centre.

**Stunning interior of the Spanish Synagogue**

The remrkable Eiffel Tower lookalike, Petřín Tower

# HISTORICAL SITES

**1 Vyšehrad**
High above the Vltava River sit the atmospheric ruins *(p130)* of Vyšehrad Castle. The complex includes a medieval royal palace as well as Prague's oldest-surviving rotunda and a 17th-century baroque fortress. It's also home to an ornate Art Nouveau cemetery that features the graves of a roster of Czech writers, artists and composers.

**2 Powder Gate**
The 15th-century Powder Gate *(p89)* was once the ornate entryway into Prague's Staré Město. The gate marked the start of the coronation route of Bohemian kings – as such, its design features lavish ornamentation and intricate late-Gothic detailing rather than any useful defensive practicalities.

**3 Old Town Bridge Tower**
Attached to one of the most iconic bridges in the world, the Charles Bridge, this 14th-century Gothic tower *(p32)* is a beloved site in Prague. The tower has borne witness to the high and lows of Czech history, and still bears visible damage received during the Thirty Years War, when marauding Swedish forces attacked the city.

**4 Petřín Tower**
Originally a lookout tower built for the Prague Jubilee Exhibition of 1891, this remarkable steel structure rises up from the heart of the city *(p46)*. Look familiar? The structure was designed to resemble the Eiffel Tower, so much so that the peak of the tower is the same height as the Eiffel. The 299 steps lead to one of Prague's finest vantage points, with views over the city and beyond.

**5 Municipal House (Obecní dům)**
This early-20th century cultural centre *(p89)* is a shimmering example of Prague's Art Nouveau architecture and a testament to the talents of a generation of Czech architects and artists,

**Medieval Powder Gate at the edge of Staré Město**

most notably Alphonse Mucha (1860-1939), the building's designer. Tours explore the splendid interior.

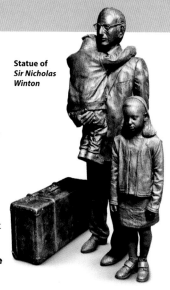

Statue of
**Sir Nicholas Winton**

## 6 Heydrich Terror Memorial

The crypt below the Church of Saints Cyril and Methodius *(p50)* houses two memorials commemorating lives lost during the Nazi occupation. The main memorial honours the seven paratroopers who participated in the assassination of Reinhard Heydrich, Nazi leader in Prague, and died in the church in 1942. The memorials are accompanied by an informative exhibit and video on the occupation years.

## 7 Sir Nicholas Winton Statue

🗺 H4  🏛 Wilsonova 300/8
🌐 nicholaswinton.com/memorials

Platform 1 of Prague's Central Station is home to a moving tribute to the man who ran the "Kindertransport" – Sir Nicholas Winton. His work saved the lives of 669 mostly Jewish children, transporting them to safety in the UK prior to World War II. This 2009 bronze statue depicts Winton carrying a little boy and standing next to a young girl.

## 8 National Memorial on Vitkov Hill

This striking monument *(p129)* to Czechoslovak statehood dates from the 1930s, and has since been subjected to the

tides of history. The Nazis destroyed large parts of the monument before the Communists used the the site to bury dignitaries, including their favourite President Klement Gottwald. The site is now owned and maintained by the National Museum, and is home to one of the largest equestrian statues in the world (of Hussite general Jan Žižka).

## 9 Prague Metronome on Letná Plinth

🗺 E1  🏛 Letenské sady, Letná

This 23-m- (75-ft-) tall metronome is a remarkable sight in and of itself, designed by sculptor Vratislav Novák as a reminder of time's unceasing flow. But the site's history only enhances its intrigue. It marks the spot where a 15.5-m (51-ft) statue of Soviet dictator Joseph Stalin stood from 1955 to 1962.

## 10 Žižkov TV Tower

Perennially featured on the "World's Ugliest Buildings" lists, and still evoking mixed feelings among Praguers to this day, this 216-m (709-ft) Communist era tower *(p130)* dominates the city skyline. Built from 1985 to 1992 in the contemporary "high-tech" style, the tower's utilitarian design has since been enlivened by sculptures of ten giant babies by Czech artist David Černý.

# MUSEUMS AND GALLERIES

**Browsing artworks at the Sternberg Palace**

Since 2000, it has also hosted a 19th-century collection. Featured in this collection are French artworks, as well as a splendid collection of Czech modern art. Other locations of the National Gallery are the St Agnes of Bohemia Convent (p40); Sternberg Palace; Schwarzenberg Palace; the Salm Palace and the Kinský Palace (p29).

## 1 Sternberg Palace
Since 1949, the fine Baroque building of the Sternberg Palace (p105) has been used to house the Prague National Gallery's collection of European art. The gallery is set over three floors that surround the central courtyard. The collection focuses on the Old Masters, and features renowned artists such as Rembrandt, Rubens, El Greco, Van Dyck, Tintoretto and Goya.

## 2 National Museum
The country's leading natural history and ethnographic museum (p122) is housed in a building that dominates Wenceslas Square. The entrance fee is worth it, if only to see the grand marble stairway, the Pantheon and the interior paintings. The annexe across the street holds rotating exhibitions.

## 3 Trade Fair Palace
**⬛ B2** **◰ Dukelských Hrdinů 47** **◷ 10am–6pm Tue–Sun** **🅦 ngprague.cz** ⬧

The National Gallery's extensive art collection is spread throughout the city in six locations. It opened its museum of 20th- and 21st-century art in 1995, and is set in a reconstruction of a Trade Fair building from 1928.

## 4 Smetana Museum
**⬛ J5** **◰ Novotného lávka 1** **◷ 10am–5pm Wed–Mon** **🅦 nm.cz** ⬧

Part of the National Museum, this grand Renaissance-style building, formerly owned by a water company, is a museum dedicated to the father of Czech music, Bedřich Smetana (p56). Documents, letters, scores and instruments detailing his life and work are exhibited here.

## 5 DOX Centre for Contemporary Art
A multi-functional space located in a former factory, DOX (p130) showcases unique works of art focusing on current social issues. It also offers special programmes for children.

## 6 The City of Prague Museum
The collection at this museum (p130) documents the history and cultural development of the Czech capital from prehistory to the 19th century when the Neo-Renaissance building was erected specially for the museum. The exhibition includes china, furniture, relics of medieval guilds, bits of famous buildings and paintings of Prague through the ages. Don't miss Antonín Langweil's

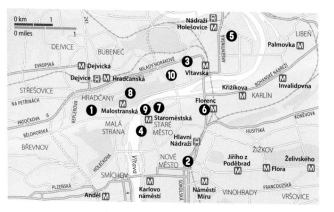

remarkable 1:500 scale model of the city, which is made entirely of paper and wood. It is a snapshot of how the city looked in 1834. The museum also manages 14 other buildings located around Prague that all house exhibitions.

# 7 Jewish Museum

First opened in 1906, the seven sites that comprise this museum *(p36)* display thousands of personal artifacts, documents and books that detail and preserve Jewish history in Bohemia and Moravia. Each of the seven sites tells a different part of the Jewish story in Prague. The museum also has a fabulous Jewish art collection.

# 8 Kunsthalle Praha

🎟 D1 🏛 Klárov 5 🕐 11am–7pm Thu–Mon, 11am–9pm Wed
🌐 kunsthallepraha.org

Located in the building of the former Zenger transformer station, this cultural and arts space presents contemporary exhibits from Czech and international artists across three galleries. The museum hosts a wide range of short-term exhibitions, educational projects, cultural events and social activities. The design shop offers a diverse selection of limited edition Czech and international design pieces in collaboration with artists.

# 9 Museum of Decorative Arts

🎟 K3 🏛 17 listopadu 2 🕐 10am–8pm Tue 10am–6pm Wed–Sun
🌐 upm.cz 🎟

The museum focuses on historical and contemporary crafts, applied arts and design. Its glass collection is one of the largest in the world, but only a fraction of it is ever on display.

# 10 National Technical Museum

🎟 F1 🏛 Kostelní 42 🕐 9am–6pm Tue–Sun 🌐 ntm.cz 🎟

This is the ultimate how-things-work museum, with exhibitions on everything from mining and metallurgy to transport and astronomy. Ask a guide to show you the coal mine.

**Exhibit at the National Technical Museum**

# WRITERS AND COMPOSERS

**1 Franz Kafka**
Although he wrote in German and almost none of his work was published in his lifetime, Franz Kafka *is* Prague. Many of his disturbing novels seem to foresee the Communist years. His work has inspired other Prague artists: look out for the giant rotating Kafka head outside Quadrio shopping centre by David Černý.

**2 Božena Němcová**
One of the greatest Czech writers of the 19th century, Božena Němcová was a founder of modern Czech prose. She was particularly interested in folklore – her work consists of short stories and more extensive prose against a rural backdrop. She is known for her novella *Babička (The Grandmother)*, regarded as a classic of Czech literature.

Author Karolína Světlá, famous for her novels

**3 Karel Čapek**
This Czech writer is best known for his science fiction and psychologically penetrating novels. With his 1920 play *R.U.R. (Rossum's Universal Robots)* he gave the world a word for an automaton, from the Czech word *robota*, meaning "forced labour".

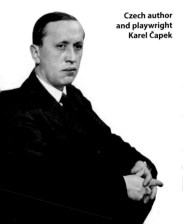

Czech author and playwright Karel Čapek

**4 Karolína Světlá**
Born in 1830, Světlá became one of the most prominent Czech authors during the 19th century. She is regarded as the founder of the Czech novel. Many of her books, including *Černý Petříček* and *Zvonečková královna*, depicted life in Prague during the 19th century and focused mainly on societal issues from that time.

**5 Jaroslav Hašek**
A notorious joker and the author of the celebrated satirical dig at the Austrian army, *The Good Soldier Švejk* (published in 1921), Hašek was also the creator of the Party for Moderate Progress Within the Bounds of the Law.

**6 Bedřich Smetana**
The composer wrote his opera *Libuše*, based on the legendary princess, for the reopening of Prague's National Theatre in 1883. Smetana vies

with Antonín Dvořák for the title of best-loved Czech composer; the former's ode to beer in *The Bartered Bride* gives him a certain advantage.

# 7 Antonín Dvořák
The works of Dvořák, such as his *Slavonic Dances*, regularly incorporate folk music. He composed his final *New World Symphony* while he was director of the National Conservatory in New York City.

# 8 Bohumil Hrabal
This poetic author used to sit in the Staré Město pub U Zlatého tygra *(p94)*, taking down the stories he heard there. His most notable works are *Closely Watched Trains*, *I Served the King of England* and *Too Loud a Solitude*.

# 9 Květa Legátová
A writer and novelist, Legátová is known for *Želary*, a collection of short stories that explore the harsh reality of early 20th-century life in a remote fictional Czech village. In 2002, she was awarded the State Prize for Literature and published *Jozova Hanule*, her autobiographical novel.

# 10 Václav Havel
The former Czech president was known as a playwright and philosopher before he became a civil rights activist protesting the Warsaw Pact invasion in 1968 *(p10)*. His absurdist works and fame helped draw international attention to the struggles of his country.

**Former Czech president Václav Havel**

# TOP 10
# WORKS OF ART, MUSIC AND LITERATURE

**1. Slav Epic**
Art Nouveau master Alfons Mucha celebrates the Czech mythic past in this cycle of 20 large canvases.

**2. The Castle**
Kafka worked on this novel of social alienation while living in Prague Castle's Golden Lane *(p23)*.

**3. The Good Soldier Švejk**
Hašek was so effective in making fun of the army and the Austro-Hungarian empire that Czechs still have a hard time taking authority seriously.

**4. Home Cook**
At the start of the 19th century, M D Rettigová became a pioneer in the field of culinary literature with this book.

**5. R.U.R.**
Karel Čapek's science-fiction play is a sometimes dark study of labour relations and social structures.

**6. The Grandmother**
Author Božena Němcová based the narrator in her 1855 novella *Babička* on her own grandmother, from whom she heard many of these stories.

**7. Vltava**
Smetana's *Má vlast (My Homeland)* is a set of six tone or symphonic poems celebrating Bohemia. The second, *Vltava*, follows the eponymous river's course.

**8. New World Symphony**
With his ninth symphony, composed in 1893, Dvořák incorporated the style of American folk songs.

**9. Disturbing the Peace**
Havel meditates on Communism and the values underlying Central Europe's pursuit of democracy in this work.

**10. The Unbearable Lightness of Being**
The novel is Milan Kundera's non-linear tale of love, politics and the betrayals inherent in both.

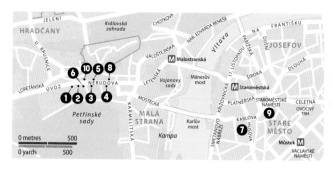

# HOUSE SIGNS

## 1 The White Swan
**🏠 Nerudova 49**

Prague houses weren't given identifying numbers until 1770, when Empress Maria Theresa brought the famed Habsburg trait of orderliness from Vienna to the banks of the Vltava. Before that, homes were known and located by a charming but confusing system of allegorical symbols. Nerudova street in Malá Strana (p96) has the highest concentration of house signs in the city. Originally many of them had local significance, although today much of their meaning has been lost. The White Swan is one of these, and probably originated as a golden goose.

## 2 The Two Suns
**🏠 Nerudova 47**

This house was once the home of the much-loved Czech poet and author Jan Neruda (1834–91), after whom

**The Two Suns house sign**

the street is named. Traditionally, this was the writers' and artists' area of Prague, and Neruda conveyed the Bohemian atmosphere of Malá Strana in his work. The connection continues today with the quarter's many small art galleries and craft shops.

## 3 The Golden Key
**🏠 Nerudova 27**

Castle goldsmiths, such as the ones who worked at this house in the 17th century, paid fees to the city, unlike their colleagues who lived in the castle's Golden Lane (p23). As such, they were entitled to advertise their wares, as preserved today in this building's façade.

## 4 The Red Lamb
**🏠 Nerudova 11**

One of the street's more unlikely symbols, the scarlet sheep adorning this façade has a significance so arcane, not even the current house owner can explain it. It remains in place as one of the city's many idiosyncrasies.

## 5 The Golden Wheel
**🏠 Nerudova 28**

This house symbol may have had something to do with alchemy – the wheel represents a stage in the *magnum opus*, the process by which the base metal lead was purportedly turned into gold.

## 6 The Green Lobster
⌂ Nerudova 43

Who knows what they were thinking when they hung the crustacean above their door – probably trying to keep up with the neighbours at the Pendant Parsnip (No 39).

## 7 Golden Tiger
⌂ Husova 17

This 15th-century house was originally decorated with a hoe, but this was changed in 1702 to a mural of a golden tiger, which still stands above the door. Most famously it was the favourite pub of the Czech author Bohumil Hrabal.

## 8 The Three Fiddles
⌂ Nerudova 12

They say a demonic trio screeches on their instruments here on moon-lit nights. The house was home to a family of violin-makers in the early 18th century, and the sign advertised their trade. Like many of the other buildings on this street, it is now home to a restaurant.

## 9 St Wenceslas's Horse
⌂ Staroměstské náměsti 16

This mural can be seen on the façade of Štorch House (also

**Mural of St Wenceslas on horseback, Štorch House**

referred to as "At the Stone Virgin Mary") located at the Old Town Square (p28). Created by Mikoláš Aleš, it acts as a tribute both to the patron saint of Bohemia and the blacksmiths who shod horses bound for the castle.

## 10 The Golden Horseshoe
⌂ Nerudova 34

The ornate doorway of this beautiful pale-blue building is adorned with an image of St Wenceslas on horseback. Below this dangles a golden horseshoe; it's likely that this was once the home or workshop of a blacksmith.

**Beautiful doorway of the Golden Horseshoe**

# MYTHS AND LEGENDS

**Representation of the Golem**

## 1 The Golem
It is said that rabbi Judah Loew *(p114)* created a clay automaton to defend the Jews of the Prague ghetto. When the creature ran amok one day, Loew was forced to deactivate him and stash him in the attic of the Old-New Synagogue *(p114)*.

## 2 Turk in Ungelt
Among the merchants who lived in the Týn settlement behind the Church of Our Lady *(p51)* was a Turkish immigrant. When his betrothed ran off and married another, he flew into a rage and chopped her head off. He is said to wander around the Ungelt courtyard carrying the decapitated head.

## 3 One-Armed Thief
The story of the thief who sought to steal jewels from a statue of the Madonna in the Basilica of St James *(p90)*, claims that the stony Virgin seized him by the arm and local butchers had to cut him loose. According to some, the thief still haunts the church asking visitors to help him fetch his arm.

## 4 Ghosts and Legends Museum
**Q** D3 **⌂** Mostecká 18
**W** mysteriapragensia.cz
Uncover old Prague's most famous mysteries and legends in this museum exploring the city's ghosts and stories. The cellar has a replica of some of old Prague's streets, while the ground floor offers more traditional exhibits that provide background to the legends.

## 5 The Iron Man
Falsely believing his fiancée to be unfaithful, a knight called off their wedding. After she drowned herself in grief, he realized his mistake and hanged himself. Every 100 years he appears in Platnéřská street to find a young virgin who will free him by talking to him for at least an hour.

## 6 The Drowned Man
In the late 19th century, young Bobeř Říma stole a bicycle and rode it into the river. If a soggy fellow tries to sell you a bike near the Staré Město end of Charles Bridge, just keep walking.

**A woodcut (1512) depicting a werewolf attack**

## 7 Werewolf

Apparently, the gamekeeper of Rudolf II became so enamoured with the wolves that roamed the castle's Stag Moat that he became one himself. Nowadays, he takes the form of a large dog and tends to chase cyclists, joggers and tourists when the whim takes him, so keep looking over your shoulder.

## 8 Emmaus Devil

In an attempt to bedevil the monks at the Emmaus Monastery (p121), Satan worked there as a cook and laced the monks' food with pepper and other spices. To this day, Czech cuisine has few piquant flavours.

## 9 Drahomíra

St Wenceslas's mother was, by all accounts, an unpleasant woman. She killed her mother-in-law and might have done in her son, too, but it is said that the gates of hell swallowed her up before she could act. She sometimes wheels through Loretánská náměstí in a fiery carriage.

## 10 The Mad Barber

When a local barber forsook his home and family after he became caught up in alchemical pursuits, his daughters ended up in a brothel and his wife killed herself. He is said to haunt Karlova and Liliova streets, hoping to return to his honest profession and make amends.

**Gothic Charles Bridge in the evening**

## TOP 10 FOLK TALES

**1. John of Nepomuk Died on Charles Bridge**
Nepomuk was already dead when he was thrown over the side of the bridge by assassins hired by the king, Václav IV (p32).

**2. Vyšehrad Castle**
While it's true that Vyšehrad (p127) was the first seat of power, its importance has been inflated by legend.

**3. Alchemists Lived in Golden Lane**
Alchemists tended to live on credit in houses in town during the reign of Emperor Rudolf II.

**4. Czechs are Believers**
In the 2021 census, over 57 per cent of Czechs identified as not having a religion. Over 30 per cent of the population did not declare.

**5. Jan Masaryk Committed Suicide**
In 1948 the foreign minister was found dead in front of Černín Palace, having "fallen" from a window, according to the Communists.

**6. There's Only One Bud**
The Czech town of České Budějovice (Budweis in German) was producing beer before the US brewer, but didn't register its copyright on the name.

**7. The Danube Flows through Prague**
It's incredible how many visitors think the Danube flows through the Czech capital. The river here is the Vltava.

**8. Absinth Will Affect Your Mind**
The amount of wormwood in the drink is negligible is not enough to cause negative changes.

**9. Czechs and Slovaks are the Same Nation**
Despite centuries of shared history and continued affiliation, Czechs and Slovaks have distinct languages, cultures and traditions.

**10. Prague is the New Left Bank**
After the Velvet Revolution, some proclaimed Prague "the Paris of the 90s", due to the number of expats.

*Clockwise from top right*
**Plain exterior of the towering Basilica of St James; intricate Baroque relief of apostle St Anthony of Padua; stunning frescoes and decoration above the nave of the church**

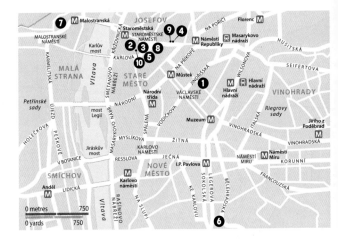

# ECCENTRIC PRAGUE

**1 Museum of Senses**
Challenge your senses at this museum (p122), where nothing is as it seems. Walk through a jungle in a tunnel where the river flows upwards or stand on top of a skyscraper and step into a desert. The amazing optical illusions here create a fun experience for the entire family.

**2 Marionette Don Giovanni**
Mozart premiered his opera *Don Giovanni* in 1787 at Prague's Estates Theatre (p73). Of the two marionette homages to the city's favourite opera, the better production

**Entrance of the National Marionette Theatre**

takes place at the National Marionette Theatre (p73). The technique of the puppeteers is so masterful, you'll leave looking for strings attached to passersby.

**3 Pragulic**
🗺 L4 🏠 Staroměstské náměstí 4
🌐 pragulic.cz
This unusual social enterprise enables you to experience the world from the perspective of homeless people, challenge stereotypes and gain insight into their daily life. Walking tours are organized by guides among the homeless and visitors can choose between short two-hour tours or a 24-hour one.

**4 Gallery of Steel Figures**
🗺 M4 🏠 Celetná 15
🕐 10am–10pm daily
🌐 galerieocelovychfigurin.cz
At this gallery, enjoy an interactive and original exhibition inspired by more than 100 characters from cartoons, sci-fi or pop culture. The figures here are made from recycled steel parts. There is also a souvenir shop and a café.

# 5 Sex Machines Museum

**L4** **Melantrichova 18**
**10am–11pm daily** **sexmachines
museum.com**

An exhibition in a slightly different
sense, this is one show that's definitely
not for kids. The museum traces the
history of instruments for sexual
gratification, from their origins to
the modern day. While not entirely
without cultural merit, the overall
package is rather bizarre.

# 6 Folimanka Underground Bunker

**Pod Karlovem Street** **Hours vary,
check website** **hrytfolimanka.cz**

This bunker, with an extensive maze of
corridors and rooms, was built during
the Cold War as a refuge for civilians
in case of any nuclear threat. There's
also an exhibition with photos of other
civilian bunkers located in Prague.
This underground bunker is open to
the public once a month on a Saturday.

# 7 Dripstone Wall

**D2** **Wallenstein Garden,
Malá Strana** **Apr–Oct: 7am–
7pm Mon–Fri, 9am–7pm Sat & Sun;
Jun–Sep: 7am–7pm daily**

This undeniably eerie wall is on the
southeastern edge of the manicured
Wallenstein Garden *(p83)*. From afar,
it looks like an enormous wall of grey
stalactites but, closer, you'll notice
haunting features hidden in the wall,
from snakes to grotesque human faces.

# 8 Museum of Torture

**M4** **Celetná 12** **10am–
10pm daily; winter: 10am–8pm daily**
**museumtortury.cz**

If you can't grasp how these grisly
instruments work, the illustrations
should make their operation painfully
clear. About 100 implements of
pain and dozens of etchings are
on display, along with explanations.

# 9 McGee's Ghost Tours

**M3** **Týnská 21** **mcgees
ghosttours.com**

Whether you are a believer or
a sceptic, the guides can guarantee
an entertaining evening as they take
you through narrow lanes and cobbled
alleys to churches and monuments.
Learn about alchemists, murderers
and the unfortunate souls who lived
here. There are three different guided
tours that last three hours each.

# 10 Idiom

**K4** **Municipal Library
of Prague, Mariánské náměstí 1**
**9am–8pm Tue–Fri, 1–8pm
Mon & Sat**

Located right by the entrance to
the Municipal Library of Prague, this
eye-catching art installation consists
of 8,000 books in a spiral – although,
thanks to some clever mirror place-
ment, it appears to go on forever.

**Haunting Dripstone Wall,
Wallenstein Garden**

Lovely landscaped Wallenstein Garden

# PARKS AND GARDENS

## 1 Petřín Hill
Stroll in the shade of trees and explore all manner of architectural quirks, from a medieval defensive wall to a mini Eiffel Tower, in one of Prague's largest green spaces (p46). In spring the views are at their best when the orchards are in bloom.

## 2 Vrtba Garden
Arguably the most beautiful in Prague, this Baroque-styled garden (p99) was designed by František Maxmilián Kaňka, who first renovated the palace for Jan Josef, Count of Vrtba, and then created the garden. It is located right behind Vrtba Palace, on the slopes of Petřín Hill (p46).

Baroque Vrtba Garden
on Petřín Hill

## 3 Wallenstein Garden
Albrecht von Wallenstein razed two dozen houses to make way for his expansive "backyard", which features an artificial lake. Among the garden's (p83) stranger elements is the grotto on the south wall, with stalactites imitating a limestone cave. The cries you hear all around you are the resident peacocks.

## 4 Kampa Island
Kampa Island is a delightfully peaceful corner of Malá Strana. Residents love to sunbathe, sip wine and play frisbee on the island green (p98) in summer. They also like to smoke marijuana, beat drums well into the night and enjoy a relaxed picnic on the island park away from the hustle and bustle of the city.

## 5 Vyšehrad
Far enough from the centre to be largely tourist-free, Vyšehrad (p127) is the perfect place to be alone with your thoughts. Sights include the Neo-Gothic Sts Peter and Paul Church, the graves of Dvořák and Smetana and reconstructed fortifications. However, visitors should be aware that there's very little shelter from inclement weather.

# 6 Stromovka

King Přemysl Ottokar II established the royal hunting park here in 1266. A public garden since 1804, Stromovka *(p128)* is one of the city's largest parks. It has four ponds that are ideal for ice-skating in winter and duck-feeding in summer and meandering paths that offer easy strolling.

# 7 South Gardens of Prague Castle

The spectacular views of Malá Strana from these castle-skirting gardens *(p22)* won't fail to inspire. Enter via the stairs from the Third Courtyard for a pleasant way to conclude a day of sightseeing in Hradčany.

# 8 Palace Gardens Below Prague Castle

This historic complex of beautiful interconnected terrace gardens is situated on the southern slopes of the Prague Castle in Malá Strana. The gardens abound in rich architectural decoration, decorative staircases, balustrades, scenic terraces, garden-houses and pavilions.

# 9 Franciscan Garden

Stop here after pounding the pavements of Wenceslas Square

**Singing Fountain in the Royal Garden**

and join the pensioners and office workers at lunch, quietly filling the benches behind the Church of Our Lady of the Snows *(p43)*.

# 10 Prague Castle Royal Garden

These formal gardens were laid out on the orders of the Habsburg king Ferdinand I in 1534 *(p105)*. After admiring Queen Anne's summer palace and the Communist-revised frescoes in the Ball Game Hall, slip down to the Stag Moat *(p106)*.

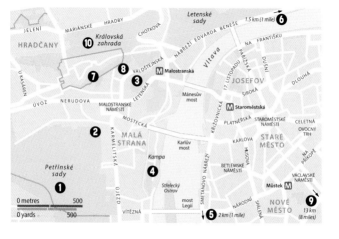

# OFF THE BEATEN TRACK

**Upside-down horse statue by David Černý**

## 1 David Černý's Upside-Down Horse Statue

🅾 N6 🅰 Štěpánská 61 ⏰ 8am–midnight daily 🌐 lucerna.cz

Works by Czech installation artist David Černý can be seen around the city, but this hanging statue of St Wenceslas astride an upside-down horse in the central passage of the Palác Lucerna is worth a special look and a laugh. It is a gentle parody of the pompous horse statue at the top of Wenceslas Square.

## 2 Cubist Lamppost

🅾 M6 🅰 Jungmannovo náměstí

The city of Prague was a hotbed of architectural experimentation in the 20th century, enthusiastically embracing the application of Cubist design concepts to all manner of buildings and objects, including – apparently – lampposts. The only one of its kind in the world, this street light can be found on a corner between Václavské náměstí and Jungmannovo náměstí.

## 3 Fantova Kavárna

🅾 H4 🅰 Wilsonova 80 🌐 fantova-havarna.cz

The old part of Prague's main train station, Hlavní nádraží, is a beautiful building. Head upstairs from the grand concourse to admire the opulent 1909 Art Nouveau Fantova

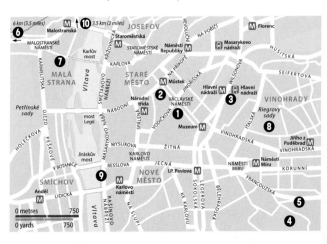

An audio-visual exhibit at the Karel Zeman Museum

Kavárna, named after the station's architect. The ambience and the beautiful interiors of the renovated station can be appreciated while sipping coffee at the café.

### 4 Grebovka
**D** B6 **A** Havlíčkovy sady 2188
**O** 10am–10pm daily
**W** pavilongrebovka.cz

Vinohrady was once covered by vineyards (that's what the name means). This pleasant gazebo in a park south of Náměstí Míru is all that's left, but it is still a wonderful place to spend a sunny afternoon sipping wine in the open air.

### 5 Krymská
**D** C6 **A** Vršovice

Prague's hipster scene is thriving along this pleasantly dilapidated street in the district of Vršovice. There are several good cafés and bars, where modern trends and old Prague clash to fascinating effect.

### 6 Divoká Šárka
**D** A5

This expansive nature reserve offers a touch of wilderness within a short tram ride of the centre. There are rugged rock formations, deep forests and even a refreshing stream-fed swimming pool during the summer months. The hilly meadows are a great spot for kite-flying in autumn.

### 7 Karel Zeman Museum
**D** D3 **A** Sashý dvůr, Malá Strana **O** 10am–7pm daily
**W** muzeumharlazemana.cz

This interactive museum focuses on the work of renowned Czech filmmaker Karel Zeman, who directed several noteworthy Czech fantasy films, including *The Fabulous World of Jules Verne* and *The Fabulous Baron Munchausen*.

### 8 Riegrovy Sady
**D** H5

This sprawling park, partly designed in the style of an English garden, offers plenty of room to spread a blanket and admire views out over the Staré Město with Prague Castle in the distance.

### 9 Náplavka
**D** E6 **A** Nové Město

The Vltava's eastern bank south of the National Theatre has come into its own as the go-to summer venue, and offers visitors everything from music festivals to farmers' markets.

### 10 Hotel International
**D** B5 **A** Koulova 15
**W** internationalprague.cz

Despite spending 40 years under Communism, central Prague has little architecture to show for it. This impressive Socialist-Realist palace – a 1950s gift from the Soviet Union – is a reminder. Check out the period-piece lobby decor.

A herd of giraffes at the popular Prague Zoo

# FAMILY ATTRACTIONS

## 1 Prague Zoo

Located on a rocky slope north of the centre overlooking the Vltava, the Prague Zoo (p127) was founded in 1924. It is home to more than 5,000 animals representing close to 700 species, 50 of which are extremely rare in the wild. There are 12 pavilions, including Hippo House, Bird Outlands, Elephant Valley and a Children's Zoo.

## 2 Public Transport Museum

⚑ A1 🏛 Patočhova 2 🕐 9am–5pm Sat & Sun 🌐 dpp.cz/muzeum-mhd

This museum located in the former Střešovice tram depot celebrates more than 150 years of Prague's transport systems. Exhibits include more than 40 historic vehicles from horse-drawn carriages to various types of trams, buses and maintenance vehicles. Other exhibits include models, photographs, historical documents, tickets, drawings and route maps.

## 3 Puppet Shows

Puppetry is a long-standing Czech tradition, and late afternoon shows will keep your children entertained for up to an hour. There's enough action that younger folk usually don't mind not understanding the libretto or narration. Weekend presentations of well-known fairy tales at the National Marionette Theatre (p73) can fill up quickly, so book in advance.

## 4 DinoPark

⚑ OC Galerie Harfa 🕐 Hours vary, chech website 🌐 dinopark.eu

Located on the roof of the Harfa Shopping Centre near Českomoravská metro station, DinoPark is the perfect place for all inquisitive minds. This attraction includes models of static and robotic life-sized dinosaurs, a palaeontological playground for kids, 4D cinema and much more.

## 5 National Technical Museum

Located in a huge hanger-like hall, this excellent, hands-on museum (p55) is sure to be a hit with kids. Inside there are vintage cars and steam trains to clamber on, a mock coal mine and a working TV studio.

## 6 Railway Kingdom

⚑ B6 🏛 Stroupežnického 23, Smíchov 🕐 9am–7pm daily 🌐 railroad-hingdom.com

The miniature world of the Railway Kingdom has dozens of model trains and cars, hundreds of metres of track, replicas of important buildings in the Czech Republic, plus an exhibition which features a unique interactive model of Prague at a 1:1000 scale.

## 7 Botanical Garden Troja

This garden is spread out over 30 ha (74 acres) and includes the historic vineyards of St Clara, a Japanese meditation garden and the unique tropical greenhouse Fata Morgana. Kids should take the cartoon map and see if they can solve the puzzle by finding 14 interesting plants and affixing stickers of them onto the correct sections.

## 8 Black Light Theatre
🗹 K4 🏛 Divadlo Ta Fantastika: Karlova 8

There are many black-light shows at theatres *(p72)* around the Staré Město, but the best one is at Divadlo Ta Fantastika. The brilliant displays should keep youngsters mesmerized.

## 9 Boat Trips
While adults might enjoy the old-fashioned rowing boats, children will prefer the splashing, pedalling action of the miniature paddleboats on the Vltava. Numerous vendors rent boats and sell tickets near the National Theatre *(p120)*. Take all the usual precautions to ensure that no one goes overboard.

## 10 Mirror Maze
The warped mirrors here are great fun for making faces, pointing fingers at elongated bodies and giggling hysterically. For older children interested in a bit of gore and history combined, the battle-scene diorama is another of the many attractions on Petřín Hill *(p46)*.

**Inside the fascinating Mirror Maze in Petřín Park**

## TOP 10 SPECIALITY STORES FOR KIDS

### 1. Marionettes under the Bridge
🏛 U Lužického semináře 7

An assortment of traditional wooden Czech puppets are on offer at this chain.

### 2. SPARKYS dům hraček Juliš
🏛 Václavské náměstí 22

This multi-level store has an excellent selection of toys, games and gifts that will appeal to all kids.

### 3. Loutky
🏛 Nerudova 51

Everything from hand puppets to antique puppets can be found here.

### 4. Agátin svět
🏛 Sokolovská 67, Karlín

Agatha's World offers a range of educational toys for kids of all ages.

### 5. Hugo chodí bos
🏛 Vodičkova 35, Nové Město

This shop has a lot to offer, from classic, locally made Czech toys to educational games.

### 6. Lego Museum
🏛 Národní 31

More megastore than museum, this city centre attraction has toys galore.

### 7. Kouzelné Hračkářství
🏛 Lesnická 6, Smíchov

Magic Toy Shop is a place full of toys, clothes and creative sets for children.

### 8. Space 4 Kids
🏛 Vinohradská 21, Vinohrady

This shop is known for its range of kids furniture sourced from around the world.

### 9. U Mostu
🏛 U Lužického semináře 5

Shop for handmade souvenirs here, made with love and inspired by Prague.

### 10. Hračky U Zlatého lva
🏛 Celetná 32

Find all sorts of toys for little ones including handmade wooden toys, children's puzzles and dolls in traditional folk costumes.

# PERFORMING ARTS VENUES

**1 State Opera**
Set at the top of Wenceslas Square next to the National Museum is the Státní opera *(p120)*. Originally known as the New German Theatre, it was built to rival the National Theatre. It offers a repertoire heavy on Italian and Viennese favourites.

**2 Divadlo Archa**
P3 Na Poříčí 26
divadloarcha.cz
The premiere venue for avant-garde theatre in Prague, Divadlo Archa has hosted artists such as David Byrne and Compagnie Pál Frenák.

**3 Hybernia Theatre**
P4 Náměstí Republiky 4
hybernia.eu
Housed in a former monastery, this theatre opened in 2006 with the musical *Golem*. It hosts a range of cultural events.

**4 Ponec**
C6 Husitská 24a, Žižkov
divadloponec.cz
This contemporary dance and movement theatre space, opened in 2001, has all aspects covered, from top international dance acts to workshops for young talent.

**5 Smetana Hall**
P3 Náměstí Republiky 5
foh.cz
The glorious Art Nouveau Smetana Hall at the Municipal House is home to the Prague Symphony Orchestra (Fok). Prague Spring Music Festival *(p84)* traditionally opens here with Smetana's *Má vlast (p57)*.

**6 The New Stage**
K6 Národní třída 4
narodni-divadlo.cz
A variety of themes involving dance, music, pantomime, black light and multimedia projections are used by the actors of Laterna Magika to bring alive stories on the stage.

**7 National Theatre**
The Národní divadlo curtain first went up for Smetana's *Libuše* in 1883; you can still see this or other Czech operas on the same stage. Go to a performance to appreciate the artistic work that went into creating the theatre *(p120)*.

**Neo-Classical façade of
the Estates Theatre**

## 8 Estates Theatre

🅟 M4 🏛 Ovocný trh 1
🅦 narodni-divadlo.cz

Stavovské divadlo is well known as the venue where Mozart's *Don Giovanni* saw its first performance. It was also the first Czech-language playhouse in what was then a largely German-speaking city. The productions occasionally leave something to be desired, but if you don't see the *Don* here, then where?

## 9 Rudolfinum

🅟 K2 🏛 Alšovo nábřeží 12
🅦 rudolfinum.cz

The Rudolfinum is home to the Czech Philharmonic Orchestra. Between 1918 and 1939, and for a brief period after World War II, the Rudolfinum was the seat of the Czechoslovak Parliament.

## 10 National Marionette Theatre

🅟 L3 🏛 Žatecká 1

The National Theatre's puppet stage represents the pinnacle of this genre, staging wonderful productions of Czech fairy tales and other shows (in Czech). They have the best Beatles tribute in town and a marionette version of *Don Giovanni* (p64).

**A performance at
the National Theatre**

## TOP 10
## CHURCHES FOR MUSIC RECITALS

**1. St Cajetan Church**
🅟 C2 🏛 Nerudova 22
This magnificent Baroque church regularly holds concerts of Bach, Mozart or Brahms.

**2. St Agnes of Bohemia Convent**
This medieval convent *(p40)* regularly holds recitals of classical music.

**3. St Nicholas Church, Malá Strana**
Appreciate the Malá Strana church's Baroque grandeur *(p98)* at a concert of sacred music.

**4. Basilica of St James**
This active house of worship *(p90)* is famous for its organ concerts and regularly invites the general public to hear the 18th century organ, which includes 8,277 pipes.

**5. Mirror Chapel**
The Baroque chamber of the Clementinum *(p90)* hosts string quartets and other small ensembles.

**6. St Martin in the Wall**
🅟 L6 🏛 Martinská 8
This Gothic church was once part of the Staré Město defences. Today the excellent acoustics of the church make this a great place to enjoy organ and other recitals that appear on the bill.

**7. Spanish Synagogue**
The ornate 1880 organ figures in the classic music concerts held in this opulent synagogue *(p113)*.

**8. St George's Basilica**
The choral and string recitals here *(p23)* present the greatest works of Mozart, Beethoven and others.

**9. Church of Sts Simon and Jude**
🅟 L1 🏛 U Milosrdných
Catch an ensemble of the Prague Symphony Orchestra players in this Renaissance sanctuary.

**10. St Nicholas Cathedral, Staré Město**
The Staré Město church *(p91)* hosts chamber music recitals twice daily and performances by the Czech Philharmonic Orchestra.

# NIGHTS OUT

Crowds around the bar at the always lively Cross Club

**1 Traditional Czech Pubs**
Prague is filled with many excellent centuries-old pubs, nearly all of which are home to great beer and good vibes. Get a taste for the city's favourite tipple, Pilsner Urquell, at U Pinkasů (upinkasu.cz) or rub shoulders with locals in the historic halls of U Fleků (en.ufleku.cz).

**2 Cabaret**
Be transported back decades by an evening of high-energy artistic cabaret. At Hybernia Theater (p72) cabaret, modern circus, vaudeville and burlesque come together in a dazzling display that could rival the Moulin Rouge in Paris.

**3 Cellar Bars**
Join the locals underground at one of Prague's famous cellar bars. Most bars serve a variety of popular beers but Andělský Pivovar (andelskypivovar.cz) brews its own (the brewing vats can be seen inside). Not a beer fan? Then step into Black Angel's Bar (blackangelsbar.com) for cocktails and cigars.

**4 Theatre**
Prague's theatre scene is incredibly vibrant yet often overlooked by visitors. See iconic plays, Czech opera and ballet at the National Theatre (p120), or visit the historic Estates Theatre (p73) where Mozart debuted his opera *Don Giovanni*. Want something more unusual?

Try "black theatre" at Ta Fantastika Theatre (tafantastika.cz) where silent shows use light on a black backdrop to tell stories.

**5 Soak in a Beer Spa**
Prague loves beer so much that it's now become a therapeutic treatment. No we're not joking, the hops and barley supposedly have health benefits. Still don't believe us? Then head to the Original Beer Spa (beerspa.com) and relax in the tubs of hops while you enjoy a glass of the finished product.

**6 Ghost Tours**
Give yourself a scare and learn of the spooky stories and tall tales that enliven Prague's history. Head down narrow alleys on an immersive evening walking tour with McGee's Ghost Tours (p65) or trade ghostly tales for dingy dungeons with Prague Underground Tours (prague-underground-tours.com).

**7 Swanky Cocktail Bars**
Just because Praguers love a beer, doesn't mean they don't also enjoy a cocktail. Sample the classics at the iconic Bukowski's bar (Bořivojova 689/86) or discover a weird range of cocktails, including whisky-infused penicillin, at hip Groove Bar (groovebar.cz).

# 8 Night Clubs

There's a club for all in Prague, no matter whether you like a bit of disco, rave or just cheesy classics. The Roxy *(p93)* is a staple and continues to pump out jungle and dub from big-name DJs. M1 Lounge *(m1lounge.com)*, meanwhile, is the place to be for RnB, both modern and old-school.

# 9 Live Music

Every night, Prague throbs to the sound of live music of every genre. Jazz lovers should hit the riverside Jazz Dock *(jazzdock.cz)*, where a variety of world-class jazz is played nightly. For a more eclectic experience, try Palác Akropolis *(p132)*. This is the heart of the indie and world-music scene and has hosted the likes of the Pixies, Apollo 440 and Transglobal Underground.

# 10 On the Water

The calm waters of the Vltava are the perfect way to see Prague by night. Prague Boats *(prague-boats.cz)* offers a range of tours – by electric boat – that are suitable for families. Alternatively, the river is the perfect place to spend an evening revelling, whether on a sunset cruise or party boat (the Bukanyr music boat is recommended; *bukanyr.cz*).

**Looking over Staré Město and the Vltava at night**

## TOP 10
## LIVE MUSIC CLUBS

**Reduta jazz club**

### 1. Reduta
Reduta *(p123)* is all about jazz performances – Bill Clinton even played sax here.

### 2. U Malého Glena
This intimate club *(p102)* pairs world-class music with a relaxed vibe.

### 3. Ungelt
🚇 M3 🏛 Jilská 1a
Head underground to enjoy jazz and blues with occasional funk and fusion.

### 4. AghaRTA
Local and international acts perform at this medieval Gothic cellar *(p93)*.

### 5. Jazz Republic
This family-owned venue offers great food and nightly performances by incredible jazz musicians *(p93)*.

### 6. Lucerna Music Bar
Lucerna's 80s and 90s weekend nights keep pumping out the retro classics *(p123)*.

### 7. Jilská 22
🚇 L4 🏛 Jilská 22
It's all about EDM at this hip venue that specializes in dance music.

### 8. Futurum Music Bar
🚇 D6 🏛 Zborovská 82/7
This spacious venue hosts acts from almost any genre you can think of.

### 9. Klub FAMU
🚇 E4 🏛 Smetanovo nábř. 2
Find your new favourite local artist at this basement venue.

### 10. U Staré paní
🚇 L5 🏛 Michalská 441/9
Enjoy classy cocktails and smooth jazz at this throwback cocktail bar.

# PRAGUE DISHES

Nakládaný hermelín, a firm
favourite in pubs

## 1 Nakládaný hermelín

Creamy with an edible rind, this soft
cheese is marinated in oil with some
pepper, garlic and spices. The main
component of this is *hermelín*, the
Czech Camembert. A popular bar
snack, this is best enjoyed with dark
Czech bread and a cold beer.

## 2 Knedlíky

These doughy dumplings are the
side dish of choice for many gravy-
laden Czech dishes. In addition to the
savoury varieties, made with bread,
potato or bacon (*špekové*), *knedlíky*
also come stuffed with fruit (*ovocné
knedlíky*), the most popular variety
being plums (*švestkové*).

## 3 Guláš

Not as spicy as its Hungarian cousin,
Czech goulash is a rich beef stew minus
the vegetables. It's always served with
*knedlíky* (dumplings), usually made
from a mix of bread and potato. Beef
forms part of the standard recipe for
this staple dish, but you can sometimes
find goulash using venison, pork and
even vegetarian variants.

## 4 Řízek

The traditional Czech take on
schnitzel is a flattened pork cutlet,
covered in flour, egg and breadcrumbs,
then fried and served with potato
salad. Many pubs offer a chicken or
veal alternative, with chips on the side.

## 5 Utopence

These pickled sausages,
slightly sour, fatty and always piled
high with pickled onions, are an ideal
accompaniment to the local beer, as
a lunchtime or early evening snack.

## 6 Smažený sýr

Like fried mozzarella sticks, this
battered block of deep-fried mild
cheese is usually served with French
fries (*hranolky*) and a tartar sauce.
As with much of Czech cuisine, try
not to think about the cholesterol.

## 7 Halušky

The Germans call these plump little
noodles *spaetzle*. They are included in
the Czech culinary canon as a nod to
nearby Slovakia, from where they ori-
ginate. You can order them *s zelím* (with
sauerkraut) or *s bryndzou* (with a creamy,
sharp cheese). The dish is a filling and
pocket-friendly alternative to pasta.

Slovakian Halušky
with cabbage and bacon

**Svíčková na smetaně, a Czech meat dish**

## 8 Svíčková na smetaně

This is goulash's sweet cousin: slices of pot-roasted beef tenderloin are served in a carrot-sweetened cream sauce, topped with a dollop of whipped cream and cranberries. Apparently, this was one of President Václav Havel's favourite dishes. Like goulash, it's unthinkable to eat it without the *knedlíky* to mop up the sauce.

## 9 Vepřoknedlozelo

*Vepřové, knedlíky a zelí* – pork, dumplings and sauerkraut – are heavy on fat but big on flavour like true Czech soul food. Order it instead of goulash and impress your waiter with how acclimatized you are, assuming you pronounce it right, of course.

## 10 Rohlíky

The workhorse of the Prague diet, these ubiquitous banana-shaped bread rolls are served up to accompany the main meal at breakfast, lunch and dinner. Dip them in soft cheese or your dish's sauce, spread them with pâté or order them with a hot dog on nearly every street corner.

## TOP 10 CZECH BEERS

**1. Staropramen**
The hometown favourite has a light, fruity flavour. Brewed in the Smíchov district, its popularity owes as much to marketing as it does to local pride.

**2. Pilsner Urquell**
The best-known Czech beer on the international market comes from the town of Plzeň, 80 km (50 miles) south-west of Prague. It has a hoppy flavour.

**3. Krušovice**
Rudolf II established the Krušovice brewery, which produces this sweet and somewhat flat beer. Try the syrupy dark *(tmavé)* variety.

**4. Budvar**
Brewed in the town of České Budějovice, the beer is no relation to the American Budweiser.

**5. Velkopopovický Kozel**
This strong, smooth beer is well worth seeking out – some consider it the world's finest.

**6. Bakalář**
Countryside lager brewed in Rakovník, 50 km (30 miles) west of Prague.

**7. Gambrinus**
Brewed by Pilsner Urquell, this is the best-selling beer in the country.

**8. Bernard**
This unpasteurized beer has a distinct, bittersweet flavour.

**9. Únětické**
This popular microbrew from a small family-run brewery can be hard to find but worth the effort.

**10. Svijany**
The brewery produces dark and light beers, including Svijanský Máz lager.

**Staropramen beer**

Patrons enjoying their drinks in U Fleků

# BARS AND KAVÁRNAS

**1 U Fleků**
The city's oldest brewing pub, dating to 1499, U Fleků (p124) is famous for its delicious dark lager and somewhat more than modest prices. Despite what anyone might tell you, the Becherovka shots are not complimentary and the rounds will keep coming until you say "ne" five times. Very popular with tourists, and not without reason.

**2 Café Slavia**
Across from the National Theatre and on a busy river thoroughfare, Café Slavia (p94) with its 1930s Art Deco interior is a famous literary café. Theatregoers, actors and playwrights frequent this café. Enjoy a coffee and dessert at the end of the day or after a night at the theatre, admiring the view of the riverside, Charles Bridge and Prague Castle.

**3 U Zlatého tygra**
This legendary pub (p94), famed as the haunt of the late writer Bohumil Hrabal (p57), serves the finest mug of Pilsner Urquell in Prague. Apart from the Pilsner beer, the brief menu features the famous beer cheese, snacks and coffee. Regulars were indifferent when Václav Havel brought Bill Clinton in for a cold glass when they were both serving presidents, so don't expect them to take much interest in you.

JOSEFOV

DLOUHÁ

Staroměstská Ⓜ ŠIROKÁ PAŘÍŽSKÁ

⑤

KAPROVA

KŘIŽOVNICKÁ STAROMĚSTSKÉ NÁMĚSTÍ

PLATNÉŘSKÁ ⑨ CELETNÁ

KARLOVA ⑥ STARÉ MĚSTO OVOCNÝ TRH

NÁBŘEŽÍ ③ HUSOVA RYTÍŘSKÁ NA PŘÍKOPĚ

SMETANOVO ⑧ BETLÉMSKÉ NÁMĚSTÍ NA PERŠTÝNĚ VÁCLAVSKÉ NÁMĚSTÍ

Ⓜ Můstek

② NÁRODNÍ TŘÍDA Národní třída Ⓜ

④ 420 m (460 yd) SPÁLENÁ JUNGMANNOVA

OSTROVNÍ VODIČKOVA

NOVÉ MĚSTO

MASARYKOVO NÁBŘEŽÍ VYŠEHRADSKÁ ① SPÁLENÁ VODIČKOVA ŠTĚPÁNSKÁ

KARLOVO NÁMĚSTÍ ŽITNÁ

0 metres 400

0 yards 400 JEČNÁ ⑩

### 4 Café Savoy
With its Art Nouveau interiors and Neo-Renaissance style high ceiling, Café Savoy (p103) is considered one of the most gorgeous and stylish cafés in Prague. Set near the Kampa park and Petřín Hill, just a few steps from the Vltava river, this café provides the perfect setting to enjoy breakfast or lunch in a grand style. The regularly changing seasonal menu includes a variety of salads, roast meats and Czech specialities. Enjoy your coffee with one of their classic Czech desserts.

### 5 Kenton's
This is one of Prague's best cocktail bars. It may look like a Jazz Age time capsule, but Kenton's (p93) is actually a relative newcomer, and highly welcome at that. You'll find no bottle juggling, just serious mixology, very dry martinis and, if you're lucky, a seat. It remains open until 3am. You can also learn a few bartender's tricks at the regular mixology classes.

### 6 U Tří Růží
This good Czech restaurant and microbrewery (p94) feels just right for the middle of Staré Město. The decor includes several murals depicting the history of brewing in Czech lands. Beers brewed on the premises include a standard light, a dark lager, a Vienna red – from caramelized malt – and a wheat beer. The downstairs area can be crowded and noisy. Reservations are advised.

### 7 Grand Café Orient
Located on the first floor of the famous House of the Black Madonna, this café (p94) was designed during the Cubist movement in 1912 by Josef Gočár. Patrons will love the building's architecture and be fascinated by the tower of cakes that greets them at the entrance. Grand Café Orient serves tea, breakfast and lunch menus, as well as wine and cocktails.

### 8 Hemingway Bar
This is an old-fashioned cocktail bar (p93) exactly as it should be, with formally dressed barmen polishing up the glassware before they pour you the perfect Old Fashioned or Whiskey Sour. The cocktail menu has hundreds of classic mixes, and even a small selection of premium Czech, French and Swiss absinthe. Book ahead or you're likely to be turned away.

### 9 Black Angel's
This bar (p93), located in the second basement of hotel U Prince, features 1930s-style decor among original Gothic and Romanesque stonemasonry. Sip on the excellent cocktails in the sophisticated interior, while enjoying fabulous views of the Old Town Square and city centre.

### 10 Pivovarský dům
Excellent, rustic Czech fare. The house brewmaster is always concocting new flavours for his drinks, such as coffee lager or champagne ale. This is a good place (p124) to visit if you prefer herbal or fruity flavoured beers such as cherry, nettle and coffee. You can also see the fermenting vats making beer, if the process of brewing interests you.

**The dining room at the popular Pivovarský dům**

# SHOPS AND MARKETS

**1 Botanicus**
Here *(p92)* you'll find oils and salts for that hot bath your travel-weary feet crave, as well as perfumes, candles, soaps and every natural health and beauty product you can imagine. There are two branches right next to each other just off the Old Town Square.

**2 Hračky U zlatého lva**
This centrally located, multistorey toyshop *(p92)* stocks a huge selection of traditional Czech wooden toys, most of them locally produced. There's a Krtek (Little Mole – the most popular Czech cartoon character) theme through-out which will please travelling tots in search of souvenirs.

**3 Art Deco**
Enter this shop *(p92)* filled with antique furnishings, vintage clothing and one-of-a-kind knick-knacks and you'll feel you've stepped back into the First Republic. Kit yourself out in Jazz Age style, right down to the spats and cigarette holder, or dress up your parlour with an Art Nouveau clock or cordial set.

**4 Erpet Bohemia Crystal**
Set in the famous Old Town Square, this is a one-stop shop for glass and jewellery. Erpet *(p92)* sells Bohemian lead crystal, garnet jewellery, enamel glass and chandeliers,

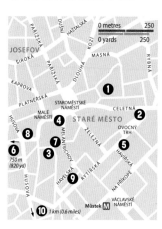

**Glass decanters at**
**Erpet Bohemia Crystal**

as well as fine goods from the Moser, Goebel and Swarovski manufacturers. Shoppers can ponder the purchases they're about to make over coffee in the shop's comfortable lounge area.

**5 Dorotheum**
🗺 M4 📍 Ovocný trh 2
Dorotheum offices throughout the world trace their roots back to the Vienna pawnbroking office, established by Emperor Josef I in 1707. As a registered member of the Association of International Auctioneers, Dorotheum holds large auctions several times a year and maintains a huge sales gallery of paintings and works of art, jewellery, silverware, glassware, fine china and furniture, as well as other collectors' items. Their regular auctions are popular with local as well as foreign clients.

**6 Artěl**
Named after a group of Bohemian artisans established in the early 1900s, Artěl *(p101)* has taken the time-honoured art of glassmaking and, working hand in hand with highly

**Exquisite and colourful cut glass items at Artěl**

skilled craftspeople, has created a collection of fresh, whimsical yet elegant designs. It has created custom designs for several top luxury brands including Burberry and Gucci.

## 7 Manufaktura

This popular gift shop chain *(p92)*, an original Czech brand, is known for offering a unique range of natural cosmetic products and accessories as well as selling traditional Czech and Moravian souvenirs. Manufaktura's line of cosmetics and attractive accessories, including scented candles, porcelain and massage tools, are ideal for a home spa.

## 8 Local Artists Praha
📍 L4 📍 Karlova 21

While walking through the "souvenir" Karlova street, set aside the time to stop at this small shop, where every item on display is a testimony to Czech traditional arts and crafts. The unique collection includes handmade pottery and beer cosmetics.

## 9 Havelské Tržiště
📍 M5 📍 7am–7pm daily

The only preserved marketplace in the Staré Město dating back to 1232. In addition to Havelská street, where the current market is located, the original one extended to Rytířská street and Uhelný trh square, which run parallel to it. It offers a selection of fresh fruits and vegetables.

## 10 Náplavka Farmers' Market
📍 E6 📍 Náplavka 📍 8am–3pm Sat
🌐 farmarshetrziste.cz

This riverfront food market is the place to be on summer Saturdays when the whole city seems to turn out to buy fresh produce, breads and meats. Even if you're not shopping, the atmosphere is infectious. Stroll the embankment and have a beer or coffee. Follow the Vltava south beyond the National Theatre to find the market.

**Náplavka Farmers' Market on the Vltava riverbank**

# PRAGUE FOR FREE

**1 Astronomical Clock**
🅥 L4 🏛 Old Town Hall
Standing below the Gothic Old Town Hall, along with hundreds of fellow visitors, marvelling at the medieval clock as it goes through its hourly procession (on the hour from 9am to 11pm) is a rite of passage. It is rather brief and admittedly underwhelming, but a must-see.

**2 Prague Castle Grounds**
🅥 C2 🏛 Prague Castle
🅦 hrad.cz
Visiting the permanent collections at Prague Castle can cost a king's ransom in entry fees. What many visitors don't realize is that it is totally free to enter the castle grounds and wander around to your heart's content. Don't miss the changing of the castle guard on the hour from 7am to 8pm (7am to 6pm in winter).

**3 Old Jewish Cemetery**
Spread across seven sites in Prague, the Jewish Museum is world class, with impressive exhibits and admission fees priced to match. If paying the full fee is beyond your budget, you can catch a small but worthwhile glimpse of the multitude of sombre tombstones in the Old Jewish Cemetery (p113) for free through a small window set in the western wall of the cemetery on Ulice 17. listopadu.

**4 John Lennon Wall**
This towering stretch of wall is covered with graffiti dedicated to Beatles frontman John Lennon. It is a relaxing – even spiritual – spot (p97). Occasionally, buskers belt out their own renditions of "Yesterday" or "Imagine". Peaceful Kampa Island (p98), a minute's walk to the east of the wall, is filled with hidden delights and well worth a wander.

**5 Vyšehrad Cemetery**
🅥 B6 🏛 Vyšehrad
🅦 praha-vysehrad.cz
The cemetery at Vyšehrad fortress (p127) is the country's most prominent burial ground and is free to enter. Fans of classical music will enjoy looking for the graves of Antonín Dvořák and Bedřich Smetana, among others. Many of the tombstones are works of art in their own right.

**6 Botanical Garden of Charles University**
🅥 F7 🏛 Na Slupi 16 🕐 10am–6pm daily; Apr–Aug: 10am–7:30pm daily 🅦 bz-uh.cz
A cosy green area in the centre of Prague, this garden opened in 1898 and gradually expanded to include an arboretum, greenhouses, ponds and a large alpine garden. It makes a pleasant place to relax.

**7 Free Walking Tours**
🅥 P4 🏛 Staré Město
🅦 extravaganzafreetour.com
This is a great way to explore Prague with a guide. Free Prague Tours is run by licensed English-speaking guides who are also history buffs.

The grave of Antonín Dvořák

**Prague's Vltava river, as seen from Letná**

Even with a generous tip at the end, you'll still save money. Tours normally begin at the Powder Gate at 11am and at Charles Bridge at 1pm.

## 8 View from Letná
**E1  Greater Prague**

Climb the steps at the northern end of Čechův most ("bridge" in Czech), north of Old Town Square for picture-postcard views of the Staré Město and the bridges traversing the river below. Keep an eye out for the metronome (p128) on the hill.

## 9 Wallenstein Garden
**D2  Malá Strana**
**Apr–Oct: 7:30am–6pm Mon–Fri, 10am–6pm Sat & Sun; Jun–Sep: 7:30am–7pm Mon–Fri, 10am–7pm Sat & Sun  senat.cz**

Malá Strana is full of Renaissance and Baroque gardens that levy a fee to enter but this lovely 17th-century garden (p66) is free to the public. The palace (p100), home to the Czech Senate, can also be visited.

## 10 Vojanovy sady
**D2  U lužického semináře 17**

Malá Strana has many green pockets, but Vojan's gardens top them all for their romantic charm. Tulip beds, flowering fruit trees and the occasional peacock add to the fairy-tale atmosphere.

## TOP 10
# BUDGET TIPS

**1.** Opera and classical music in Prague is subsidized and tickets seldom cost more than a few thousand crowns.

**2.** Consider renting a private single or double hostel room. Many hostels offer these at a fraction of the price they would cost in a hotel.

**3.** Time your stay to avoid the peak seasons around holidays, when hotel rates go through the roof.

**4.** Consider renting an apartment if you're staying for three days or longer. You'll not only save money but will have more privacy.

**5.** Buy a discounted one-day or three-day pass for Prague's public transport. These are valid for the metro, trams, buses, trains and boats. You'll save money and not have to purchase tickets for each journey.

**6.** When arriving by plane, take the municipal bus into town from the airport. A single Kč40 ticket can often get you very close to your hotel.

**7.** Resist the temptation to hop into a taxi. Most distances in the city are easily walkable, and public transport is reliable and cheap.

**8.** Eat out at lunchtime instead of dinner to take advantage of the popular three-course set menus.

**9.** Skip wine at meals in favour of beer. Czech wines can vary greatly in quality; the local beer is generally cheaper and excellent quality.

**10.** Seek out pubs in outlying districts like Žižkov, where a half-litre (pint) mug of beer can cost half the price it does in the centre.

**A classical music performance**

# FESTIVALS

## 1 Masopust
Shrove Tue

Locals dress up in masks, and sing and dance down the streets during this Czech carnival. Masopust translates to "meat-feasts" in Old Czech, alluding to the plethora of foodie feasts on offer as well. Celebrations are concentrated in the neighbourhood of Žižkov (p128).

## 2 May Day
1 May

It is customary for couples to visit the statue of the Czech Romantic poet Karel Hynek Mácha on Petřín Hill (p46). For others the national holiday is spent trying to forget the old obligatory Communist rallies.

## 3 Prague Spring International Music Festival
May–Jun

Bedřich Smetana's *Má vlast*, or *My Homeland (p57)*, kicks off the annual three-week festival that draws classical music performers and fans from around the globe. The round of concerts closes with Beethoven's Ninth Symphony.

## 4 Tanec Praha
May, Jun

This international dance festival has become an annual part of Prague's festivities. The local dance scene has greatly benefited from it, and audiences can now see contemporary productions all year round.

## 5 Karlovy Vary International Film Festival
Jul

Hobnob with the stars while you attend screenings at this festival. Hundreds of partygoers turn the sleepy west Bohemian spa town, 130 km (81 miles) from Prague, upside down for nine days.

## 6 Street Theatre Festival
Jul

*Za dveřmi* (Behind the Door) is an international street art festival that presents drama, acrobatics, parades and juggling on the streets and squares of Prague.

## 7 Bohemia International Folklore Dance Festival
Aug

This festival has been a success since its first staging in 2005. It has now

**Performers during
the Masopust carnival**

expanded beyond Prague, as DanceBohemia, and brings amateur folklore dance ensembles together from all around the world.

**8 Prague Writer's Festival**
Salman Rushdie, Susan Sontag and Elie Wiesel are just some of the internationally acclaimed authors who have attended this annual event, which takes place every spring.

**9 Signal Festival**
Oct
This annual festival of lights is one of the city's most popular events. Across four days, Prague is filled with magical artistic light displays that celebrate digital and creative culture.

**10 Mikuláš, Vánoce, Silvestr**
Dec
Christmas celebrations are largely devoid of religion, but the mulled wine starts flowing on St Nicholas's Day (6 December) and doesn't stop until the Christmas carp is all eaten and the New Year's Eve *(Silvestr)* fireworks arsenals are depleted.

**Dancers at the Bohemia International
Folklore Dance Festival**

## TOP 10
# NATIONAL HOLIDAYS

**1. Renewal of the Independent Czech State**
1 Jan
Marks the 1993 split of Czechoslovakia.

**2. Easter Monday**
Mar–Apr
Custom dictates that men give women a gentle whipping with a branch. There are calls to end this tradition.

**3. Labour Day**
1 May
Romantics lay flowers before the statue of Karel Hynek Mácha on Petřín Hill.

**4. Day of Liberation**
8 May
Plaques around town are adorned with flowers to remember those killed by the Germans in 1945.

**5. Cyril and Methodius Day**
5 Jul
The Greek missionaries *(p118)* brought both Christianity and the Cyrillic alphabet to the Slavs.

**6. Jan Hus Day**
6 Jul
Czechs commemorate one of the greatest figures of Czech history *(p29)*.

**7. Czech Statehood Day**
28 Sep
Bohemia's history is recalled on St Wenceslas Day, as most Czechs call it.

**8. Independence Day**
28 Oct
In 1918, Czechoslovakia declared itself independent of Austro-Hungary.

**9. Day of the Fight for Freedom and Democracy**
17 Nov
The anniversary of the Velvet Revolution *(p11)* is marked with candles and flowers.

**10. Christmas**
24–26 Dec
Streets fill with carp sellers and revellers drinking mulled wine.

# AREA BY AREA

| | |
|---|---|
| Staré Město | 88 |
| Malá Strana | 96 |
| Prague Castle and Hradčany | 104 |
| Josefov and Northern Staré Město | 112 |
| Nové Město | 118 |
| Greater Prague | 126 |

*Roofs of Staré Město*

# STARÉ MĚSTO

Prague's heart is a layered cake of history dating back several hundred years: the oldest of its buildings have double cellars, owing to a flood-prevention programme that buried the original streets 3 m (10 ft) beneath those that exist today. Architecturally, it embraces every epoch, from the Romanesque to the Brutalist style of the mid-1970s Kotva department store. Historically, the burghers of the Staré Město (Old Town) were ill at ease with the castle district, and vice versa, with the town being a bastion of Protestant feistiness. Staré Město is still livelier than Malá Strana and Hradčany, with cafés, clubs, restaurants and theatres that provide entertainment around the clock.

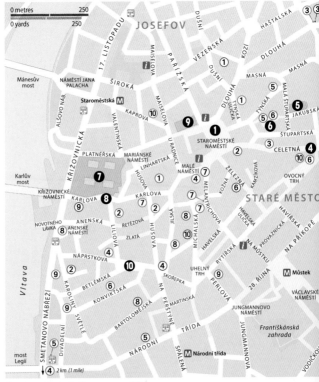

*For places to stay in this area, see p144*

Old Town Square lined with
Gothic and Baroque façades

# 1 Old Town Square

Over the centuries, this now peaceful square *(p28)* at the heart of the city has witnessed hundreds of executions, political capitulations and, more recently, riotous ice-hockey celebrations. Today, the action is more likely to come from the crowds of tourists and Praguers, enjoying a coffee or a glass of beer at a pavement café. Dominated by the Church of Our Lady before Týn *(p51)*, the square is always buzzing; in winter and summer, it's a wonderful place to watch the world go by.

# 2 Municipal House

🗺 P3 🚇 Náměstí Republiky 5
🌐 obecnidum.cz 🚻♿

National Revival artist Alfons Mucha was one of many to lend his talents to the Municipal House *(Obecní dům)*, Prague's star Art Nouveau attraction. One of its most striking features is Karel Špillar's mosaic above the main entrance, entitled *Homage to Prague*. It also has a firm place in history as it was from the Municipal House that Czechoslovakia was declared an independent state in 1918. Today, it is home to restaurants, cafés, exhibition halls, shops and the Prague Symphony Orchestra at Smetana Hall *(p72)*.

# 3 Powder Gate

🗺 P4 🚇 Náměstí Republiky
🕐 10am–7pm daily (Jul & Aug: to 9pm; Oct–Mar: to 6pm; Dec: to 8pm) ♿
In the 15th century, King Vladislav II laid the cornerstone for this tower at the city's eastern gate, intended to complement the Royal Court nearby. The name of this monument comes from its 17th-century role as a gunpowder store. The tower was damaged during Prussian attacks in 1757. The Neo-Gothic façade seen today, with its ornate sculptural decoration, dates from 1876.

1 Top 10 Sights
*p89*

1 Restaurants
*p95*

1 Cafés and Pubs
*p94*

1 Shops
*p92*

1 Nightclubs
*p93*

**Traditional house sign, Celetná**

# 4 Celetná
**⬛ M4**

The medieval route from the silver-mining town of Kutná Hora in Bohemia passed down the street known today as Celetná, through Old Town Square and on to Prague Castle.

# 5 Basilica of St James
**⬛ N3 🏠 Malá Štupartská 6
🕐 9:30am–noon & 2–4pm daily (except Mon & during Mass)
🌐 prahaina.minorite.cz**

The Gothic and Baroque interior wins the award for Prague's creepiest sanctuary. The church, founded in 1232 by Wenceslas I, is best known for the legend of the mummified arm (p60) hanging above the door. The church has excellent acoustics so make sure you don't miss the organ recitals held here.

# 6 Ungelt
**⬛ M3**

Also known as the Týn Courtyard, this was a fortified merchants' settlement in the 10th century. The Baroque and Renaissance houses were completely renovated in the early 1990s, creating what is now one of the Old Town's most charming mercantile centres.

# 7 Clementinum
**⬛ K4 🏠 Křížovnická 190, Mariánské náměstí 5 & Karlova 1
📞 222 220879 🕐 Jan–Mar: 10am–6pm daily; Apr–Sep: 9am–8pm daily; Oct–Dec: 9am–7pm daily 🔗**

Built in the mid-17th century as a Jesuit college, the Clementinum now houses the National Library. Noted astronomer Johannes Kepler discovered the laws of planetary motion atop the Astronomical Tower. There is a beautiful Baroque library, and the Mirror Chapel hosts various concerts.

## PRAGUE'S WALLS AND GATES

Prague's walls started going up in the 13th century, protecting the new settlement from the distant Tartars. The town was accessible via wall gates. As gradual developments in military technology made walls and moats less effective forms of defence, Praguers found new uses for their fortifications. The broad ramparts became parks, complete with benches, lamps and even cafés. The city kept the habit of locking its gates at night well into the 19th century, however.

## 8 Karlova

📍 K4

You will inevitably get lost trying to follow Karlova street from the Old Town Square to Charles Bridge; relax and enjoy the bewildering, twisting alleys crammed with shops and cafés.

## 9 St Nicholas Cathedral

📍 L3 📍 Staroměstské náměstí ⏲ 10am–5pm Mon–Sat, noon–5pm Sun 🌐 svmikulas.cz 📍

This Baroque jewel began as a parish church. During World War I, it was used as a garrison church for Czech soldiers. It now belongs to the Hussite Church and also operates as a concert hall.

## 10 Bethlehem Square

📍 K5 ⏲ Chapel: 9am–6pm daily 🌐 bethlehem chapel.eu 📍

The 15th-century Catholic reformer Jan Hus (p29) preached in the reconstructed chapel on the square's north side. The church was converted into apartments in the 18th century but was lovingly restored to its former state in the 1950s.

Clementinum's Baroque library, adorned with frescoes

## A STROLL AROUND STARÉ MĚSTO

### Morning

After breakfast at the **Municipal House** café (p89), take a guided tour of the building, then go and climb the **Powder Gate** (p89).

Wander down **Celetná**, ducking through the arcade to Štupartská and the **Basilica of St James**. If you have at least 45 minutes before the top of the hour, make your way through the **Ungelt** courtyard to the **Old Town Square** (p28). Join a tour of the **Old Town Hall** and get a backstage view of the Apostles' show on the **Astronomical Clock** (p82). Otherwise, spend some time shopping in the Ungelt, then join the crowd below the clock outside to see the spectacle. For lunch, head slightly out of the square to **Pasta Fresca** (p95).

### Afternoon

Return to the Old Town Square, then enter the meandering turns of **Karlova** and wander past the area's old buildings before turning south to reach **Bethlehem Square**. Take a tour of the Bethlehem Chapel. If you'd like a break, have a beer at **U Zlatého tygra** (p94), a three-minute walk north, then retrace your steps to Karlova to visit the **Clementinum**.

After freshening up, take in a concert or a performance at the theatre. Curtains go up around 7:30pm, so dine afterwards.

Shoppers at Prague's famous Palladium mall

# Shops

## 1. Amadea
**L4** **Melantrichova 6**
Find a wide range of wooden products such as ornaments, decorations, souvenirs, utensils and kitchenware, all hand-picked by the owners.

## 2. Moser
**M4** **Staroměstshé náměstí 15**
Browse through classic crystal and cut-glass objects produced by this well-known manufacturer.

## 3. Palladium
**P3** **Náměstí Republiky 1**
One of the most popular shopping destinations in downtown Prague, Palladium has 200 shops offering exciting shopping and dining experiences to visitors.

## 4. Erpet Bohemia Crystal
**L4** **Staroměstské náměstí 27**
Located across from the Astronomical Clock, this megastore has an exclusive collection of Bohemian crystal, art glass, fine costume jewellery, crystal figurines and much more. The staff are friendly and attentive.

## 5. Material
**M3** **Týn 1, Ungelt**
Czech tradition in designer crystal and glassware gets a modern makeover at this shop in the Ungelt courtyard. Admire the eye-catching stemware, vases, dishes and candle-holders, all presented in a space that fuses classical and modern design.

## 6. Botanicus
**M3** **Týn 2 & 3**
The store's all-natural health and beauty products are produced at a "historic village" east of Prague; enquire about tours. Herbs, oils and other seasonings are also sold here.

## 7. Manufaktura
**L4** **Melantrichova 17**
This is a one-stop shop for all your small souvenir needs, including Czech folk crafts and traditional wooden toys. In addition to these items, there are also naturally made cosmetics and toiletries featuring an odd assortment of ingredients, such as Czech beer, wine and thermal salt.

## 8. Art Deco
**L4** **Michalshá 21**
Come here for a range of goods including handbags, jewellery, ceramics, glassware and vintage clothing inspired by the early 20th century.

## 9. Český Porcelán
**M5** **Perlová 1**
Bohemian porcelain might not be as prestigious as Bohemian crystal, but it makes a pretty souvenir or present.

## 10. Hračky U zlatého lva
**N4** **Celetná 32**
Explore the range of traditional wooden toys and other board games here (p80).

# Nightclubs

## 1. Kenton's
**L2** **V Kolkovně 3** **hentons.cz**
One of Prague's fancier bars, Kenton's has a classy vibe with an elegant interior and a wooded counter. There's a good range of interesting cocktails.

## 2. Hemingway Bar
**J5** **Karolíny Světlé 26** **hemingwaybar.cz**
Inspired by Ernest Hemingway, the great author and one of the most well-known bar lovers, this place offers his favourite liquors such as Absinthe, a variety of rum, champagne, and excels in mixology.

## 3. Roxy
**N2** **Dlouhá 33** **roxy.cz**
In addition to the best dance parties in town, this club hosts experimental theatre and live bands.

## 4. Jazz Republic
**M6** **Jilská 1a** **jazzrepublic.cz**
One of Prague's top music clubs, Jazz Republic features live jazz, funk, blues, dance, Latin, fusion or world music seven nights a week.

## 5. Vagon
**L6** **Národní třída 25** **vagon.cz**
One of the originals for exciting live music, this place hosts blues or rock bands most nights, with a mix of well-known and emerging talents.

A band performing at the popular nightclub, Roxy

Classic bar with shelves of drinks at Black Angel's Bar

## 6. AghaRTA Jazz Centrum
**M4** **Železná 16** **agharta.cz**
Named after Miles Davis's seminal album from the 1970s, this club has daily performances by top Czech musicians and hosts the annual AghaRTA Prague Jazz Festival.

## 7. Black Angel's
**L4** **Staroměstské náměstí 29** **blachangelsbar.com**
Designed in the style of a Prohibition era speakeasy, this attractive bar offers creative drinks and cocktails.

## 8. Friends
**K6** **Bartolomějská 11** **friendsclub.cz**
Prague's best gay cocktail bar has a steady following among expats and locals. Evenings are filled with a rich mix of DJ sets, karaoke and themed parties or quizzes.

## 9. Zlatý Strom
**K4** **Karlova 6** **zlatystrom.com**
Enjoy unusual views of the Prague night sky through the glass ceilings of this subterranean club. There are two dance floors inside.

## 10. Caffrey's
**M3** **Staroměstské náměstí 10** **caffreys.cz**
This lively Irish bar is one of the most popular in town. The beer terrace in front of the pub offers the perfect setting to enjoy drinks during summer.

# Cafés and Pubs

### 1. Café Obecní dům
🗺 P3 📍 Náměstí Republihy 5
🌐 havarnaod.cz
Stop for breakfast at this café with Art Nouveau interiors, before setting off for a day exploring Staré Město.

### 2. U Tří Růží
🗺 L5 📍 Husova 10 🌐 u3r.cz
This charming 15th-century brewery and restaurant, on Husova street, serves on-site brewed beers and a menu of Czech classics.

### 3. Lokál Dlouhááá
🗺 N2 📍 Dlouhá 33 🌐 lokal-dlouha.ambi.cz
Rumoured to serve the city's freshest Pilsner Urquell beer, delivered to the door in big tanks.

### 4. Terasa U Prince
🗺 L4 📍 Staroměstské náměstí 29
🌐 terasauprince.com
Visit this café and restaurant on the rooftop terrace of Hotel U Prince for a truly memorable dining experience.

### 5. Café Slavia
🗺 J6 📍 Národní třída 1 🌐 cafeslavia.cz
Set in the historical centre of Prague, this café offers Czech and international cuisine that include salads, fish and meat specialities.

### 6. Grand Café Orient
🗺 N4 📍 Ovocný trh 19
🌐 grandcafeorient.cz
With its Cubist style decor, the specialities at this elegant café include the traditional Czech pastry, *kubistický věneček*.

### 7. U Zlatého tygra
🗺 L4 📍 Husova 17 🌐 uzlatehotygra.cz
Located in the heart of Staré Město, this pub is renowned for its old world charm and Pilsner beer.

### 8. Prague Beer Museum
🗺 J5 📍 Smetanovo nábřeží 22
🌐 praguebeermuseum.cz
This is one of the four branches of this popular pub with around 30 Czech beers on tap.

### 9. Atmosphere
🗺 J5 📍 Smetanovo náb. 14
🌐 atmosha.cz
This café, pub and restaurant offers its customers tank beer, Italian and Czech wines, plus various Czech dishes.

### 10. Café Ebel
🗺 L3 📍 Kaprova 11 🌐 ebelcoffee.com
You won't find a better cup of coffee in the city than at Ebel, which uses beans from all over the world. It is not far away from the Old Town Square (*p28*).

**Diners on the rooftop terrace of Terasa U Prince**

# Restaurants

Interior of Maitrea, a popular restaurant

## 1. Maitrea
📍 M3  🏠 Týnská ulička 6
🌐 restaurace-maitrea.cz · ⓀⓀ
Located just off the Old Town Square, Maitrea is an excellent vegetarian and vegan restaurant, which serves traditional Czech fare alongside Mexican, Thai and other international dishes.

## 2. Wine O'Clock
📍 K4  🏠 Liliová 16  🕐 Sun & Mon
🌐 wineoclockprague.com · ⓀⓀ
Enjoy tasty Italian small plates, from bruschetta pomodoro to aubergine parmiggiana, with a glass of wine at this cozy establishment.

## 3. Pasta Fresca
📍 M4  🏠 Celetná 11  🌐 pasta-fresca.net · ⓀⓀⓀ
Chef Tomáš Mykytyn makes regional Italian dishes with seasonal ingredients. Sommeliers are on hand to guide diners through the wine menu.

## 4. V Zátiší
📍 K5  🏠 Liliová 1  🌐 vzatisi.cz · ⓀⓀⓀ
Sample modern and unconventional versions of traditional Czech and international dishes at this well-established fine dining restaurant.

## 5. Divinis
📍 M3  🏠 Týnská 21  🕐 Sun
🌐 divinis.cz · ⓀⓀⓀ
This high-end wine bar and restaurant manages to balance a modern feel with a traditional Italian atmosphere. Good-quality wines complement the classic Sicilian specialities.

## 6. Sad Man's Tongue
📍 K6  🏠 Konviktshá 7  🌐 sadmanstongue.com · ⓀⓀ
This popular bar and bistro serves up a big helping of Americana in the heart of Prague.

## 7. Bistro Monk
📍 L4  🏠 Michalshá 20
🌐 bistromonk.cz · ⓀⓀ
Prepared from local produce, the food at Bistro Monk is simple and delicious. Try the pancakes with blueberry sauce.

## 8. Hosarowa
📍 L5  🏠 Jilshá 6  🌐 hosarowa.business.site · ⓀⓀ
Come here for Prague's best Korean barbecue, along with other classics like bibimbap and garak-guksu.

## 9. Století
📍 N2  🏠 Karolíny Světlé 21
🌐 stoleti.cz · ⓀⓀ
Try dishes named after Czech artists, writers and singers in a simple but stylish dining room. The menu has a good list of vegetarian options.

## 10. Plzeňská restaurace Obecní dům
📍 P3  🏠 Náměstí Republiky 5
🌐 pivniceod.cz · ⓀⓀ
Classic Czech food is served in a lively setting here. The extensive à la carte menu features dishes such as roast duck and grilled ribs.

# MALÁ STRANA

Founded in 1257, Malá Strana (the Little Quarter) is built on the slopes below the castle hill with magnificent views across the river to Malá Strana. Floods, fires and war kept construction going on the Vltava's left bank; very few of the original Romanesque and Gothic buildings remain. During the reign of the Habsburgs, grand palaces were built in Baroque style, and today many of these serve as parliament or government buildings and embassies. The area is filled with quaint churches and dominated by beautiful Baroque buildings that flank the winding streets, which rise steeply away from the river and lead to splendid views of Petřín Park. In between the streets are small squares adorned with some of the city's grandest structures and home to the best dining options in Prague.

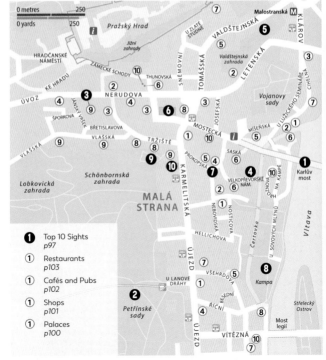

**1** Top 10 Sights
p97

**1** Restaurants
p103

**1** Cafés and Pubs
p102

**1** Shops
p101

**1** Palaces
p100

*For places to stay in this area, see p145*

The iconic Charles Bridge over the Vltava river

# 1 Charles Bridge

For almost all visitors to Prague, this spectacular Gothic bridge (p32), crossing the Vltava from the castle complex to the Staré Město, remains their most memorable image of the city long after they have returned home.

# 2 Petřín Hill

A more than welcome respite from the maze of tiny, generally crowded streets in the city below is this sprawling park looking down over spires and rooftops. Enjoy the views all the way up the hill by taking the funicular (p47).

# 3 Nerudova
**⚑ C2**

A picturesque narrow street lined with former palaces, Nerudova leads uphill from Malostranské náměstí's winding side streets to Prague Castle (p22). It is named after 19th-century Czech writer and poet Jan Neruda (1834–91) who lived in the House of the Two Suns. Traditionally an artists' quarter, the street is worth exploring for its many craft shops and galleries. It is also home to one of the most concentrated collections of historic house signs (p58) in the city.

# 4 John Lennon Wall
**⚑ D3 ⬢ Velhopřevorské náměstí**

Prague's street artists and the secret police once waged a long-running paint battle here, as the latter constantly tried to eradicate the graffiti artists' work (p82). The original artwork, created by students after Lennon's assassination, has been painted over many times, but the John Lennon Peace Club still gathers annually at this self-made shrine to sing the former Beatle's praises – and his songs.

# 5 Wallenstein Garden
**⚑ D2 ⬢ Apr–Oct: 7am–7pm daily**

Laid out in the grounds of the Baroque Wallenstein Palace (p118) these gardens have not changed since they were created by Duke Albrecht of Wallenstein in the 17th century. The garden's most notable features include a series of magnificent bronze statues and a loggia decorated with scenes from the Trojan War.

A bronze sculpture at Wallenstein Garden

## 6 St Nicholas Church
**C2** **Malostranské náměstí** **Hours vary, chech website** **stnicholas.cz**

In the early 18th century, Jesuits constructed this stunning example of Baroque architecture on the site of a former Gothic parish. This prominent Prague landmark was designed by the acclaimed father and son Baroque architects, Christoph and Kilian Dientzenhofer, while other leading artists adorned the interior with exquisite carvings, statues and frescoes. From the 1950s the clock tower often served as an observation and spying point for the state security. For an extra fee, you can climb the tower for a memorable view over the orange rooftops of Malá Strana.

## 7 Maltézské náměstí
**C3**

The Knights of Malta once had an autonomous settlement here, and the square still bears their name. Search for the Bench of Václav Havel in the centre of the square. Hiding just a few steps from the square to the east is the 12th-century Church of Our Lady below the Chain, whose name refers to the chain used in the Middle Ages to close the monastery gatehouse.

## 8 Kampa Island
**D3–4**

The tiny Čertovka (Devil's Canal) that separates Kampa from Malá Strana was once the town's "laundry", milling area and, in the 17th century, home to a thriving pottery industry. A popular park now covers the island's southern end, while the northern half is home to elegant embassies, restaurants and hotels.

Formal flower beds
of the Vrtba Garden

## A DAY IN MALÁ STRANA

### Morning

You can approach the Little Quarter from Staré Město as royal processions once did, by crossing **Charles Bridge** (p32), or you can save your energy for the day ahead, and start from the top of the hill and walk down. Get to **Nerudova** (p97) from one of the many side streets leading from Hradčany and stroll down, window shopping at the many craft outlets on your way. As long as you go downhill, you'll end up at the area's central hub, **Malostranské náměstí**. Here, spend at least an hour admiring **St Nicholas Church**. Pause for lunch at a café on Malostranské náměstí.

### Afternoon

After lunch, take Tomášská to the **Wallenstein Garden** (p66). Tiptoe through the tulips at **Vojanovy sady** (p83) and continue down U lužického semináře under Charles Bridge and onto the lovely **Kampa Island**. Explore the island, then head off to check the writing on the **John Lennon Wall** (p82) before visiting the **Church of Our Lady Victorious** and finally enjoy the magnificent evening views from the highest point of **Vrtba Garden**.

In the evening, relax at the Bench of Václav Havel in the middle of Maltézské náměstí, or head to **U Malého Glena** (p102) to relax while listening to jazz and blues.

## 9 Vrtba Garden

🗺 C3   🏛 Karmelitská 25
🕐 Apr–Oct: 10am–6pm daily
🌐 vrtbovsha.cz

Enjoy magnificent views of Prague Castle and the Malá Strana from the highest point of this beautiful Baroque garden laid out by architect František Maximilián Kaňka in about 1720.

## 10 Church of Our Lady Victorious

🗺 C3   🏛 Karmelitská 9   🕐 Church: 8:30am–6pm Mon–Sat, 8:30am–7pm Sun; Museum of the Infant Jesus of Prague: 9:30am–5pm Mon–Sat, 1–6pm Sun

Also known as the Church of the Infant Jesus of Prague, Prague's first Baroque church (1611) got its name and its Catholic outlook after the Battle of White Mountain (p9). Visitors flock to see the church's miracle-working statue of the infant Christ (p50).

**Lavish Baroque interior of
St Nicholas Church**

# Palaces

### 1. Nostitz Palace
**D3** **Maltézské náměstí 1**

Take in the restoration work at this 17th-century palace while enjoying a chamber music concert. The palace now serves as the seat of the Czech Ministry of Culture.

### 2. Thun-Hohenstein Palace
**C2** **Nerudova 20**

The Kolowrat family's heraldic eagles support the portal of this palace. Built by Giovanni Santini-Aichel in 1721, the building is now home to the Italian Embassy.

### 3. Liechtenstein Palace
**C2** **Malostranské náměstí 13** **amu.cz**

Originally several different houses, the Liechtenstein Palace fused in the 16th century. Today, it is home to Prague's Academy of Music and hosts concerts and recitals.

### 4. Morzin Palace
**C2** **Nerudova 5**

The two giant Moors (hence Morzin) bearing up the Romanian Embassy's façade are said to wander about Malá Strana streets at night.

### 5. Wallenstein Palace
**D2** **Valdštejnské náměstí 4** **10am–6pm Sat** **senat.cz**

General Wallenstein pulled out all the stops creating what is essentially a monument to himself. On the palace's frescoes, the Thirty Years' War commander had himself depicted as both Achilles and Mars.

### 6. Buquoy Palace
**D3** **Velkopřevorské náměstí 2**

This pink stucco palace and the John Lennon Wall are separated by only a few steps, but they are miles apart aesthetically. The French Ambassador helped preserve the graffiti.

### 7. Michna Palace
**C4** **Újezd 40**

Francesco Caratti modelled this palace on Versailles in the 17th century. It is home to the Sokol Physical Culture Movement.

### 8. Schönborn Palace
**C3** **Tržiště 15** **schoenbrunn.at**

Count Colloredo-Mansfeld owned the palace in the 17th century: having lost a leg in the Thirty Years' War, he had the stairs rebuilt so he could ride his horse into the building.

### 9. Lobkowicz Palace (Převorovských)
**B3** **Vlašská 19** **lobkowicz.cz**

Home to the German Embassy. In 1989 hundreds of East Germans found their way to the West by scrambling over the back fence of this embassy building.

### 10. Kaunitz Palace
**C3** **Mostecká 15**

The Yugoslav (now Serbian) Embassy sat quietly in its pink and yellow stucco palace for more than 300 years until war made it a popular spot for protests.

**The picture gallery at Nostitz Palace**

Lovely entrance of Květinářstvi u Červéneho Iva

# Shops

### 1. Bel Art Gallery
**C3** **Karmelitshá 26**
This small fine art gallery and shop, set in a 17th-century building, sells contemporary paintings, sculptures and ceramic works from more than 30 acclaimed artists. International shipping is available.

### 2. Shakespeare a Synové
**D3** **U Lužichého semináře 10**
This bookstore specializes in foreign books and several titles in English, German and French. It offers a space for literary readings and discussions.

### 3. Muzeum Slivovice R. Jelínek
**D2** **U Lužichého semináře 48**
**muzeumslivovice.cz**
Head to the shop of this distillery museum to pick up a bottle of *slivovice*, a traditional Czech plum spirit. Book a tasting to sample it before buying.

### 4. Curiomat
**B2** **Nerudova 45**
Just under New Castle Steps, this small shop sells original Czech puppets, gifts, toys, ceramics, jewellery, art and enamel tableware.

### 5. Artěl
**D3** **U Lužichého semináře 7**
This store is known for exquisite mouth-blown and hand-engraved glassware and crystalware for decor of unique design motifs.

### 6. Květinářstvi u Červéneho Iva
**D3** **Sashá**
It appears as if a jungle is sprouting from the hole in the wall that is the Flowershop at the Red Lion. Spruce up your apartment or hotel room with their unique arrangements.

### 7. Perníkový panáček
**D2** **Cihelna 2a**
Located near the entrance to the Franz Kafka museum, this little side-street bakery has all manner of gingerbread creations, which make for great gifts.

### 8. Malostranské starožitnictví
**C2** **Malostranské náměstí 28**
This antiques store is a treasure trove of jewellery, watches, porcelain objects, silverware, coins and photographs. It also sells musical instruments.

### 9. Designum Gallery
**C2** **Nerudova 27**
This design boutique offers the works of up-and-coming artists apart from the established brands and designers. The highlights at the boutique include glass, porcelain as well as contemporary jewellery.

### 10. Orel and Friends
**C2** **Nerudova 6**
A wide selection of traditional Czech crafts, including ceramics, jewellery, handbags, leather-bound books and more, are available at this unique store.

# Cafés and Pubs

**Lovely Beatles-themed interior of the Wall Pub**

## 1. Bakeshop Little Bakery
🅿 D2  🅰 U Lužichého semináře 22
This little bakery serves pastries, breads, quiches and desserts. It also has a daily changing menu of fresh juices, smoothies and homemade soup served with croutons.

## 2. Café Kafíčko
🅿 C3  🅰 Maltézské náměstí 15
This café, with its excellent coffee and homemade cakes, proves to be the perfect getaway from the cold of the winter or the summer crowds.

## 3. Baráčnická rychta
🅿 C3  🅰 Tržiště 23
This wood-panelled beer hall, housed in a Modernist 1930s building, is a little piece of traditional Czech Republic in Malá Strana.

## 4. Cukrkávalimonáda
🅿 C3  🅰 Lázeňská 7
Located opposite the entrance to the Church of Our Lady below the Chain, this popular little patisserie is all about three things: *cukr* (sugar), *káva* (coffee) and *limonáda* (lemonade).

## 5. Alebrijes
🅿 D2  🅰 U Lužichého Semináře 109/38  🆆 alebrijescocina mexicana.com/general-1
Come to this cosy restaurant and bar for a relaxed meal with friends and family, and enjoy traditional Mexican drinks and cuisine.

## 6. U Kocoura
🅿 C2  🅰 Nerudova 2
You might think the regulars at this pub on Malá Strana's main drag would be used to tourists by now, but don't be surprised if every face turns to meet you. It serves excellent Pilsner.

## 7. Kofárna Café
🅿 D4  🅰 Zborovská 60
In addition to excellent coffee, Kofárna offers many plant-based food options too. Try the famous Israeli hummus.

## 8. Café Bella Vida
🅿 D4  🅰 Malostranské nábřeží 3
This café serves its own coffee blend as well as delectable mini-desserts and sandwiches. Sit in the cosy garden and enjoy the beautiful views of Charles Bridge and Prague Castle.

## 9. U Malého Glena
🅿 C3  🅰 Karmelitská 23
🆆 malyglen.cz
Prague's smallest jazz venue, "At Small Glen's", also has a cosy restaurant where you can enjoy a variety of food and brunch at weekends.

## 10. The Wall Pub
🅿 D3  🅰 Hroznová 495/6
Less than a minute's walk from the John Lennon Wall, this pub is all about celebrating the legendary singer. Enjoy steaks and burgers in the garden.

# Restaurants

### 1. Cantina
🚩 C4 🏠 Újezd 38 🌐 cantinana brezi.cz · ⓀⓀ
The fajitas here are great; choose from chicken, beef, pork or shrimp.

### 2. Augustine Restaurant
🚩 D2 🏠 Letenská 12/33 🌐 augustine-restaurant.cz · ⓀⓀⓀ
This restaurant serves European cuisine prepared with seasonal ingredients and a wide selection of drinks.

### 3. Malostranská Beseda
🚩 C2 🏠 Malostranské náměstí 21
📞 257 409112 · ⓀⓀ
Set in an elegant building in the heart of Little Quarter, this cosy place serves traditional Czech food and beer.

### 4. Czech Slovak Restaurant
🚩 C4 🏠 Újezd 20 🌐 czech slovah.cz · ⓀⓀⓀ
This place brings traditional Czech and Slovak dishes into the 21st century in an artistic fashion.

### 5. Ichnusa Botega Bistro
🚩 D4 🏠 Plashá 5 📞 605 375012 · ⓀⓀⓀ
A family-run bistro which offers a delicious range of Sardinian dishes.

### 6. Kampa Park
🚩 D3 🏠 Na Kampě 8b 🌐 hampapark.com · ⓀⓀⓀ
This top riverside restaurant serves Continental classics and fusion cuisine.

### 7. Terasa U Zlaté studně
🚩 C2 🏠 U Zlaté studně 4 🌐 terasa uzlatestudne.cz · ⓀⓀⓀ|
With its picturesque views, this fine dining restaurant offers the perfect setting to celebrate special occasions with friends and family.

### 8. Coda Restaurant
🚩 C3 🏠 Tržiště 9 🌐 coda restaurant.cz · ⓀⓀⓀ
Enjoy the stunning views from the rooftop terrace of the Aria Hotel while sampling delicious Czech dishes.

### 9. St Martin
🚩 C3 🏠 Vlašská 7 🌐 stmartin.cz · ⓀⓀ
Try traditional Czech dishes alongside Asian twists on American classics.

### 10. Café Savoy
🚩 C4 🏠 Vítězná 5 🌐 cafesavoy.ambi.cz · ⓀⓀⓀ
This feels just like a Prague café should, with high ceilings and huge windows.

**Patrons at the busy Café Savoy**

# PRAGUE CASTLE AND HRADČANY

Founded by Prince Bořivoj in the 9th century, Prague Castle and its attendant cathedral tower overlook the city from the long hill known as Hradčany. The surrounding town was founded in 1320, becoming home to servants' hovels and, after the cataclysmic fire of 1541, grand palaces. Renaissance and Baroque reconstructions in the area created much of what visitors see today. At the castle, primitive defences were removed, making room for gardens, parade grounds and the other needs of a modern empire. When the Habsburgs moved the imperial seat to Vienna, Hradčany seemed to become preserved in time. The area abounds with interesting sights for art and history lovers, as well as hidden lanes and parks – in short, a total expression of the Czech nation's shifting epochs and politics.

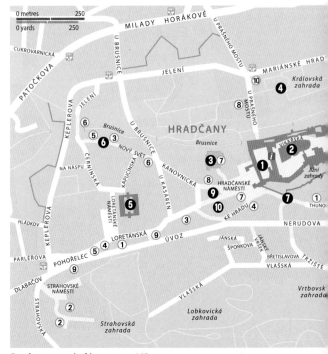

*For places to stay in this area, see p145*

**A Bronzino painting at the Sternberg Palace**

# 1 Prague Castle

The first and main focus of most tourists' visit to the city of Prague is the majestically located and architecturally varied castle complex (p22). Its determined survival in the face of an often turbulent history seems only to heighten the castle's lure for visitors. Despite its medieval appearance, it is still as much of a political stronghold as it has always been, and currently serves as the office of the country's president.

# 2 St Vitus Cathedral

The Gothic splendour of St Vitus's (p26) spires can be seen from almost every vantage point in the city, but don't miss the opportunity to see its beautiful stained-glass windows and imposing gargoyles up close.

# 3 Sternberg Palace

**▣ B2 ◨ Hradčanské náměstí 15**
This fine Baroque building, dating from 1698, houses the National Gallery's collection of European art from the classical to the Baroque. Spread over three floors, it is without doubt the country's best collection from the period. Its highlights include works by Rubens, Rembrandt and El Greco.

# 4 Royal Garden

**▣ C1 ◨ U Prašného mostu
◨ Apr–Oct: 10am–dusk daily
☑ hrad.cz**
This garden was originally laid out in 1534 by Ferdinand I. Although today's visitors may regret the disappearance of the maze and the pineapple trees that once featured here, they are likely to appreciate the absence of Rudolf II's freely roaming lions and tigers. In the English-style garden are the former presidential residence (the First Lady didn't like it), the *sgraffitoed* Ball Game Hall and Queen Anne's Summer Palace (Letohrádek královny Anny), also known as the Belvedere.

**❶** Top 10 Sights
p105

**①** Restaurants
p109

**①** Cafés and Pubs
p108

**Beautiful ceiling frescoes in the Loreta**

### 7 New Castle Steps
📍 C2

The Royal Route, established in the 15th century for the coronation of George of Poděbrady, covered the distance from the Municipal House on Náměstí Republiky *(p89)* to the castle. The last stretch of steps climbed the hill here at the Zámecké schody.

### 8 Old Castle Steps
📍 D2

The comparatively gentle slope of the Staré zámecké schody – the castle's "back door" entrance – leads from the Malostranská metro to the citadel's eastern gate. Local artists and artisans line the steps, selling

### 5 Loreta

The onion-domed white towers of this Baroque 17th-century church *(p34)* complex are like something out of a fairy tale.

### 6 Nový Svět
📍 A2

Nestled below Loreta *(p34)*, at the head of the Stag Moat, is Nový Svět (New World), the best street in town for a romantic stroll. The low houses were built in the 17th century to replace slums built for castle workers after their houses burned down in 1541. They have been spruced up, but are otherwise unspoiled. Rudolf II's choleric astronomer Tycho Brahe lived at No 1.

---

**STAG MOAT**

When the Stag Moat was not fulfilling its defensive duties, Prague's rulers used it as a hunting park. Rudolf II is said to have been particularly fond of chasing deer around the narrow, wooded gorge with his pet lions. The Powder Bridge's earthworks were excavated to permit pedestrians access to both halves of the moat.

everything from watercolour prints to polished stones.

# 9 Hradčanské náměstí
☑ B2

Many visitors enter this square backwards, trying to fit St Vitus's spires into their photographs. Tear your eyes away from the castle's western face and you'll see, among other Renaissance buildings, the colourful Archbishop's Palace and the Schwarzenberg Palace opposite, housing the Bohemian Baroque art of the National Gallery. In the green centre is a plague column from 1726; opposite the castle is the Toskánský Palace, now part of the Ministry of Foreign Affairs.

# 10 Schwarzenberg Palace
☑ B2

An inherent part of the Prague Castle panorama, Schwarzenberg Palace is a significant Early Renaissance building. Its façade is elaborately decorated with *sgraffito* patterns. The permanent exhibition here presents a selection of excellent masterpieces from the Old Masters collection.

**Small cottages on
Nový Svět in Hradčany**

## A DAY IN HRADČANY

### Morning

Start your day with a brisk climb up the **New Castle Steps**, then take a leisurely stroll through the grounds. When you're ready, leave the castle behind and walk west through **Hradčanské náměstí**; time your exit for the Changing of the Guard at noon. Next, head to the **Schwarzenberg Palace** and take time to browse some Baroque Czech art. Alternatively, treat yourself to the Old Masters collection at **Sternberg Palace**.

Afterwards, walk up **Loretánská** to **Loretánské náměstí**, where you'll find the vast **Černín Palace** staring down at **Loreta** (p34). Explore the pilgrimage site and its odd gallery of saints before having lunch at **Kavárna Nový Svět** (p108).

### Afternoon

Exit Loretánské náměstí past the Capuchin monastery and follow Černínská downhill, pausing on **Nový Svět** lane. Admire the street's charming piebald houses and follow Kanovnická street back to Hradčanské náměstí.

The rest of the afternoon will be taken up with a tour of the unmissable **Prague Castle** (p22), **St Vitus Cathedral** (p26) and other attractions in the castle complex.

To end your sightseeing day in Hradčany, find your way back to the famed pub **U Černého vola** (p108) at Loretánské náměstí 1 for a generous mug of beer.

# Cafés and Pubs

### 1. U Černého vola
**A2** ⚐ Loretánské nám. 1
"At the Black Ox" is one of the original Old Prague beerhalls. Watching the regulars knock back litres of beer, you can guess why it's so popular.

### 2. Pivovar Strahov
**A3** ⚐ Strahovské nádvoří 301
Located in the Strahov Monastery founded by Vladislav II in 1142, this place brews three unfiltered, unpasteurised beers on tap year-round.

### 3. Mandlárna
**B2** ⚐ Loretánská 5
W loretanska.mandlarna.cz
Besides its delicious almond recipes, this café has everything from syrups and pastries to liquor. Try the speciality *Mandlokáva*, espresso with almonds.

### 4. Starbucks Pražský hrad
**B2** ⚐ Hradčanské náměstí – Kajetánka
Sip an espresso on the rooftop while peering at Prague through one of the telescopes. The quiet patio has large tables where you can enjoy lunch.

### 5. Kavárna Nový Svět
**A2** ⚐ Nový Svět 2 W havarna.novysvet.net
At this small family café, try soup or salad for lunch, or just sit with a good cup of coffee and enjoy the atmosphere.

### 6. Romantik Hotel U Raka
**A2** ⚐ Černínská 10
The Hotel U Raka at the far western end of Nový Svět is a striking half-timbered building, an unusual sight in the urban Czech Republic. Enjoy a coffee in cosy surroundings.

### 7. Mezi řádky
**B2** ⚐ Hradčanské nám. 15
Situated in the Sternberg Palace, this is a good spot to enjoy a cup of coffee and a light snack after visiting the castle.

### 8. Gallery Café
**B2** ⚐ U Prašného mostu 53
This café and gallery is situated at the Powder Bridge in the former Jízdárna (Riding School) building. Outdoor seating is available. Visitors can enjoy stunning views of the Stag Moat *(p106)*.

### 9. Café Melvin
**A3** ⚐ Pohořelec 8
Set in a 15th-century house at the beginning of the Royal Route, this café serves a range of beverages, home-made desserts and sandwiches.

### 10. Lobkowicz Palace Café
**C2** ⚐ Jiřská 3 W lobkowicz.cz
This pleasant restaurant offers light lunches and suppers with a view of the city. The café in the courtyard is a good place to end your tour of the castle.

**Outdoor terrace of the Lobkowicz Palace Café**

# Restaurants

**PRICE CATEGORIES**
For a three-course meal for one with
half a bottle of wine (or equivalent
meal), taxes and extra charges

Ⓚ under Kč500 ⒦⒦ Kč500–Kč1,000
ⓀⓀⓀ over Kč1,000

**Traditional Czech dishes
at Kuchyň**

## 1. U Krále Brabantského
🅾 C2 🏠 Thunovshá 15 🌐 hrcma
brabant.cz · ⒦⒦
Meat lovers will enjoy this medieval-
themed restaurant in a genuinely
historic setting.

## 2. Na Pekle
🅾 A3 🏠 Strahovské nadvoří 1
🌐 napehle.cz · ⒦⒦
Continental dining in a grotto under the
Strahov Monastery. Traditional Czech
meals include golden-roasted pork knee.

## 3. Vinobona
🅾 B2 🏠 Nový Svět 11
🌐 vinobona.cz · ⒦⒦⒦
Set in the enchanting Nový Svět (p106),
this bistro is a must-visit. It has delicious
breakfast and lunch choices. The chef's
degustation menu is great too, and
there's an excellent choice of wines.

## 4. U ševce Matouše
🅾 A2 🏠 Loretánské náměstí 4
🌐 usevcematouse.cz · ⒦⒦
"At the Cobbler Matouš", in a cosy, low,
vaulted room, has made an art of
melting cheese on beefsteaks.

## 5. Malý Buddha
🅾 A3 🏠 Úvoz 46 🌐 maly
buddha.cz · ⒦⒦
The "Little Buddha" serves a wide range
of potent teas and Vietnamese food.

## 6. Plzeňka Nový Svět
🅾 B2 🏠 Nový Svět 77 📞 773
781010 · ⒦⒦
This restaurant serves delicious
Czech and international dishes, and
is immensely popular with locals
and tourists alike.

## 7. Kuchyň
🅾 B2 🏠 Hradčanské náměstí 1
🌐 huchyn.ambi.cz · ⒦⒦⒦
Located in the Neo-Renaissance
Schwarzenberg Palace (p107), Kuchyň
offers homemade Czech meals inspired
by recipes from old cookbooks along
with excellent tank beer.

## 8. U Labutí
🅾 B2 🏠 Hradčanské náměstí 11
🌐 ulabuti.com · ⒦⒦
Restaurant "At the Swans" serves
up Zubr lager and some substantial
dishes, such as schnitzel and goulash.
There is seating in the courtyard.

## 9. Host Restaurant
🅾 B2 🏠 Loretánská 15 🌐 restaurant
host.cz · ⒦⒦⒦
Enjoy fine dining alongside
sweeping views of Petřín Hill
and Malá Strana.

## 10. Lví dvůr
🅾 B1 🏠 U Prašného mostu 6
🌐 restaurant-lvidvur.cz · ⒦⒦
This rooftop dining room affords great
views of St Vitus Cathedral (p26). Enjoy
Lobkowicz Premium beer alongside
delicious Czech cuisine.

*Clockwise from above*
**Overlooking Prague
from the steps
under Prague
Castle; tourists
climbing the Old
Castle Steps; statue
of Karel Hašler
"The Songster" by
Stanislav Hanzík**

# JOSEFOV AND NORTHERN STARÉ MĚSTO

It is impossible to precisely date the arrival of the Jewish community in Prague, but historical sources mention the destruction of a Jewish settlement on the Vltava's left bank in the 13th century. For the next 500 years, Prague's Jewish population was obliged to live in a walled ghetto, where the Josefov quarter is today. When Emperor Josef II removed these strictures, the ghetto turned into a slum occupied by the city's poorest population. The quarter was razed in the late 19th century, making way for avenues such as Pařížská. Now the area is home to the Jewish Museum, which showcases Prague's Jewish heritage.

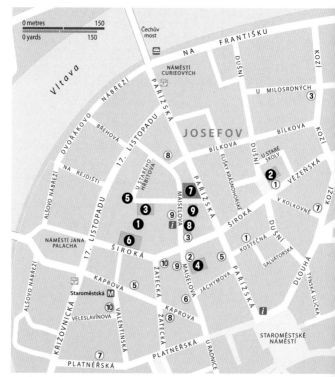

Gravestones in the
Old Jewish Cemetery

# 1 Old Jewish Cemetery

K2 ◘ Široká ◘ Apr–Oct: 9am–
6pm Sun–Fri; Nov–Mar: 9am–4:30pm
Sun–Fri ⓦ jewishmuseum.cz

The sight of hundreds of graves, their
leaning headstones crumbling on top
of each other, is a moving and
unforgettable experience – a testa-
ment to the treatment of the Jewish
people in Prague, confined to their
own ghetto even in death. Although
there is no definite record of the
number of burial sites located
here, to appreciate the depth of
the graveyard, compare the grave-
stones' height with that of the street
level on U Starého hřbitova.

# 2 Spanish Synagogue

M2 ◘ Vézeňská 1
◘ Apr–Oct: 9am–6pm Sun–Fri;
Nov–Mar: 9am–4:30pm Sun–Fri

The Moorish interior with its
swirling arabesques and stucco
decoration gives this synagogue
(p51) its name. It stands on the
site of the Old School, Prague's
first Jewish house of worship.
František Škroup, composer
of the Czech national anthem,
was the organist in the mid-19th
century. It hosts exhibitions of
Jewish history and synagogue silver.

❶ Top 10 Sights
  p113

① Cafés and Restaurants
  p117

① Shops
  p116

Arabesque façade of the
Spanish Synagogue

**Jewish exhibits, Klausen Synagogue**

## 3 Klausen Synagogue
**K2** ⬛ U Starého hřbitova 1
⬛ Apr–Oct: 9am–6pm Sun–Fri; Nov–Mar: 9am–4:30pm Sun–Fri ⬛

Abutting the Old Jewish Cemetery, this Baroque building was constructed in 1694 on the site of a school and prayer hall (klausen) where Rabbi Loew taught the cabala. It now houses Jewish exhibits, including prints and manuscripts.

## 4 Maisel Synagogue
**L3** ⬛ Maiselova 10
⬛ Apr–Oct: 9am–6pm Sun–Fri; Nov–Mar: 9am–4:30pm Sun–Fri ⬛

Rudolf II permitted Mordechai Maisel to build his private synagogue here in the late 16th century, in gratitude for the Jewish mayor's financial help during Bohemia's war against the Turks. It was destroyed by fire in 1689, but was later rebuilt as a Jewish museum (p36) in Neo-Gothic style. Inside is a wonderful collection of Jewish silverwork and other items such as candlesticks and ceramics. Ironically, during the Nazi occupation, the Third Reich planned to build a museum in Prague, dedicated to the Jewish people as an "extinct race".

## 5 Ceremonial Hall
**K2** ⬛ U Starého hřbitova 3a
⬛ Apr–Oct: 9am–6pm Sun–Fri; Nov–Mar: 9am–4:30pm Sun–Fri ⬛

Constructed in the early 1900s in striking mock Romanesque fashion, the Ceremonial Hall was home to the Jewish community's Burial Society. The fascinating exhibits housed inside detail the complex Jewish rituals for preparing the dead for the grave.

## 6 Pinkas Synagogue
**K3** ⬛ Široká 3 ⬛ Apr–Oct: 9am–6pm Sun–Fri; Nov–Mar: 9am–4:30pm Sun–Fri ⬛

After World War II, this 15th-century Gothic building with some early Renaissance features became a monument to the estimated 80,000 Czech and Moravian victims of the Holocaust – the names and dates of all those known to have died either in the Terezín camp or in others across Eastern Europe are written on the wall in a moving memorial. Equally moving is the exhibition of writings and paintings made by the children (of whom there were more than 10,000 under the age of 15) confined in Terezín (p39).

## 7 Old-New Synagogue
**K2** ⬛ Červená ⬛ Apr–Oct: 9am–6pm Sun–Fri; Nov–Mar: 9am–5pm Sun–Fri ⬛ synagogue.cz ⬛

Across the street from the cemetery, Europe's oldest surviving synagogue has witnessed a turbulent history, including pogroms and fire, and has

### RABBI JUDAH LOEW BEN BEZALEL

One of Prague's most famed residents, Rabbi Loew ben Bezalel (c 1520–1609) is associated with numerous local legends but he was also a pioneering pedagogue and a leading Hebrew scholar of the times. Foremost among the myths surrounding Loew is that of the Golem (p60), a clay automaton the rabbi supposedly created to defend the ghetto.

## A DAY IN THE JEWISH QUARTER

### Morning

A sobering place to start the day, the **Pinkas Synagogue** lists Holocaust victims and helps visitors to appreciate how large the Czech Jewish community once was. Afterwards take a stroll through the adjoining **Old Jewish Cemetery** (p113). Also worth visiting in this area is the Baroque **Klausen Synagogue**, with its exhibits on Jewish family life.

A short walk away is the **Old-New Synagogue**, where you'll find treasures like Rabbi Loew's seat. Exiting, note the **Jewish Town Hall** next door. Inside the Jewish Quarter information centre is **Café Golem** (p117), a good stop for a light lunch.

### Afternoon

After lunch, enter antiques shops en route to the **Maisel Synagogue**, where you'll find an exhibit on the Jewish settlement in Bohemia and Moravia – it continues at the **Spanish Synagogue** a five-minute walk to the east down Široká.

Refresh yourself at **Bakeshop Praha** (p116) before walking a few minutes northeast to the **St Agnes of Bohemia Convent** (p40) with its exhibits on Czech medieval art.

Finally, enjoy dinner at **5th District Restaurant and Café by King Solomon** (p117) and attend a concert of sacred music at the Spanish Synagogue.

---

often been a place of refuge for the city's beleaguered Jewish community. Its name may come from the fact that another synagogue was built after this one, taking the title "new", but which was later destroyed.

## 8 Jewish Town Hall
**🗺 L3 📍 Maiselova 18**
**🚫 To the public**

The hands of the Rococo clock on the town hall, or *Židovská radnice*, turn counterclockwise as Hebrew is read from right to left. The building was one of Mordechai Maisel's gifts to his community in the late 16th century, but it was renovated in Baroque style in 1763.

## 9 High Synagogue
**🗺 L2 📍 Červená 4 🚫 To the public**

Constructed along with the town hall with funds from Mordechai Maisel, the High Synagogue was built in elegant Renaissance fashion. Subsequent reconstructions updated the exterior, but the interior retains its original stucco vaults. Inside there are also impressive Torah scrolls and mantles.

## 10 St Agnes of Bohemia Convent

This 13th-century Gothic convent (p40) is full of spectacular wall panels and altarpieces, as well as original 13th-century cloisters and chapels. The artworks, part of the gallery's collection, comprise some of the best Czech medieval and early Renaissance art.

# Shops

### 1. Spanish Synagogue Gift Shop
**M2** **Vězeňská 1**
Exquisite torah pointers, *kabala* hands, *Hannuka menoras* (nine-branched candelabrums) and books are all on offer at this shop.

### 2. Kosta Boda
**L3** **Maiselova 12**
The tiny Josefov outpost of the renowned glassmaker has been producing glass artworks and tablewares since the mid-1700s.

### 3. Hodinářství (Old Clocks)
**L3** **Maiselova 16**
To find this small shop selling old clocks, simply stand at the corner of Maiselova and Široká streets and you'll hear the old cuckoo clock sing.

### 4. Granát Turnov
**N2** **Dlouhá 28**
Specializing in Bohemian garnet, Granát Turnov is part of Prague's biggest jewellery chain. Jewellery lovers can find a large variety of brooches and necklaces here.

### 5. Gucci
**L3** **Pařížská 9**
Treat yourself to high-end luxury fashion from this world-renowned brand. Located on the tree-lined Pařížská street, this store is one of many designer boutiques frequented by tourists and locals alike.

### 6. Drahonovsky
**M2** **Dlouhá 19**
Aficionados come to this tiny goldsmith's workshop for gold and silver jewellery, much of which is embellished with the celebrated red Bohemian garnet.

### 7. Bakeshop Praha
**M2** **Kozí 1**
Grab a bag of brownies, *rugelach* or butterhorns (small crescent-shaped

**Baked treats at the Bakeshop Praha**

biscuits) and other mouthwatering treats, or lunch on an egg salad sandwich and coffee. There are also salads and quiches to take away.

### 8. Antik Ambra
**L3** **Kaprova 12**
This serious collector's shop specializes in jewels and small decorative items such as clocks and coins. If you don't find what you're looking for, just ask and they'll point you in the right direction.

### 9. Antique Cinolter
**L3** **Maiselova 9**
Art lovers should peruse this small gallery's sale exhibition of local art. The original oils and sketches capture Josefov's bittersweet warmth and humanity.

### 10. Alma Antique
**K3** **Valentinská 7**
What don't they sell? Alma Antique is a bazaar stocked with Persian rugs, jewellery, Meissen porcelain, crystal and ornate nesting dolls. This is one of the largest antique dealers in Prague.

# Cafés and Restaurants

### 1. Krčma
**L3** **Kostečná 4** **725 157262** · Ⓚ Ⓚ
A medieval-themed tavern just off swanky Pařížská, Krčma offers reasonably priced food, draught beer and lots of low-lit ambiance.

### 2. Naše maso
**N2** **Dlouhá 39** · Ⓚ Ⓚ
The casual setting in a butcher shop makes this better suited to a quick bite. The meat is quality local beef and pork.

### 3. Field
**M1** **U Milosrdných 12** **fieldrestaurant.cz** · Ⓚ Ⓚ Ⓚ
A stylish restaurant, with an intimate atmosphere and an interesting mural projected from the ceiling. Innovative dishes and modern cuisine are served.

### 4. La Degustation Bohême Bourgeoise
**N2** **Haštalská 18** **ladegustation.cz** · Ⓚ Ⓚ Ⓚ
La Degustation, a Michelin-starred restaurant, offers tasting menus of traditional Czech cuisine.

### 5. La Bodeguita del Medio
**K3** **Kaprova 5** **labodeguita.com** · Ⓚ Ⓚ
This Cuban-Creole restaurant offers grilled fish and meats made using traditional ingredients. Popular with the business crowd, it has a great atmosphere and welcoming staff.

5th District Restaurant and Café by King Solomon

### 6. Pivnice u Pivrnce
**L3** **Maiselova 3** **upivrnce.cz** · Ⓚ Ⓚ
A pub with wall decorations by Czech caricaturist Peter Urban. Choose from Czech specialities or enjoy a beer.

### 7. La Finestra in Cucina
**K4** **Platnéřská 13** **lafinestra. lacollezione.cz** · Ⓚ Ⓚ Ⓚ
Italian favourites cooked to perfection and great wine are complemented by the fine setting and service.

### 8. Les Moules
**L2** **Pařížská 19** **lesmoules.cz** · Ⓚ Ⓚ
Enjoy oysters and mussels at this Belgian restaurant.

### 9. Café Golem
**L3** **Maiselova 15** **603 962963** · Ⓚ
This stylish little café serves great coffee, bagels, soups and cakes.

### 10. 5th District Restaurant and Café by King Solomon
**L3** **Široká 8** **Fri** **patactvrt.cz** · Ⓚ Ⓚ Ⓚ
Prague's foremost kosher restaurant has separate facilities for meat and dairy.

# NOVÉ MĚSTO

Founded in 1348, Nové Město (New Town) is hardly new. Charles IV's urban development scheme imposed straight avenues on the settlements springing up outside the old city walls and added a fourth town to the constellation of Staré Město, Malá Strana and Hradčany. Unlike Staré Město, Nové Město was a planned grid of streets and markets. The horse market became Wenceslas Square in the 19th century; the 14th-century cattle market, and Europe's largest square, took on Charles's name, becoming Karlovo náměstí.

**1** Top 10 Sights
*p119*

**1** Restaurants
*p125*

**1** Cafés and pubs
*p124*

**1** Galleries
*p122*

**1** Nightspots
*p123*

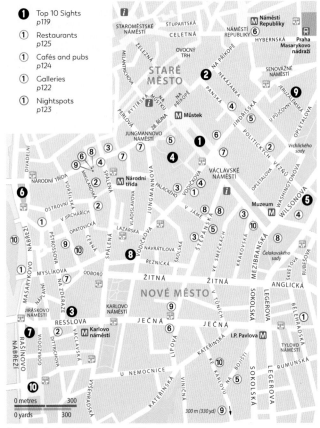

0 metres 300
0 yards 300

300 m (330 yd) **9**

*For places to stay in this area, see p146*

Wenceslas Square, Prague's bustling commercial hub

# 1 Wenceslas Square

Standing in contrast to the medieval Old Town Square (p28), the lively Wenceslas Square (p42) expresses the history of 20th-century Prague, from its many beautiful Art Nouveau façades to the memories of the numerous marches, political protests and celebrations that have shaped the city over the past 100 years.

# 2 Na Příkopě
**N5**

Formerly a moat protecting the city's eastern flank, Na Příkopě is Prague's fashion boulevard, counting Gant, Benetton, Desigual and Guess among its range of big-name stores. Shoppers jam the pedestrian zone and pavement cafés, streaming between the gleaming Myslbek shopping centre and Slovanský dům, with its ten-screen multiplex cinema. The Hussite firebrand Jan Želivský preached on the site now occupied by another shopping mall, the Černá Růže Palace.

# 3 Cathedral of Sts Cyril and Methodius
**E5 Resslova 9 9am–5pm Tue–Sun**

This Baroque church, with a pilastered façade and a small central tower, was built in the 1730s. In the 1930s, the church was given to the Czechoslovak Orthodox Church and dedicated to Sts Cyril and St Methodius, the 9th-century "Apostles to the Slavs". In 1942, the Heydrich Terror (p51) took place here. A small museum on-site tells the story of these events. In the crypt is the National Memorial to the Heroes of the Heydrich Terror – a bronze plaque has been hung on the wall in their memory.

# 4 Franciscan Garden
**N6**

The Franciscans moved here in 1604, claiming a former Carmelite monastery. The grounds and nearby Church of Our Lady of the Snows had fallen into decay after the Hussite civil war, but the monks beautifully restored them. The area was closed to the public until 1950, when the Communists thought the gardens were worth sharing. Although there's little love lost for the dictatorship of the proletariat, the garden (p43) remains popular with locals.

Heydrich Terror memorial, Cathedral of Sts Cyril and Methodius

## 5 State Opera
**⬛ G4 ⬛ Wilsonova 4**
**⬛ narodni-divadlo.cz**

The first theatre built here, the New Town Theatre, was pulled down in 1885 to make way for the present building. A Neo-Classical frieze decorates the pediment above the columned loggia at the front of the theatre. The interior is stuccoed, and original paintings in the auditorium and on the curtain have been preserved.

## 6 National Theatre
**⬛ E4 ⬛ Národní třída 2**
**⬛ narodni-divadlo.cz**

Patriotic Czechs funded the theatre's construction twice: once in 1868 and again after fire destroyed the building in 1883. To see the stunning allegorical ceiling frescoes and Vojtěch Hynais's celebrated stage curtain, take in one of the operas staged here; good picks are Smetana's *Libuše*, which debuted here, or Dvořák's *The Devil and Kate*. You can see multimedia performances at The New Stage (p72) next door.

## 7 Dancing House
**⬛ E6 ⬛ Jiráshovo náměstí 6**
**⬛ galerietancicidum.cz**

Built in 1992–6, this edifice by Vlado Milunic and Frank Gehry is known as the Dancing House, or "Ginger and Fred", due to its iconic towers, which resemble two dancers. Most of the building is now a hotel owned by former Czech international football player, Vladimír Šmicer. The two tower rooms, with their castle and Vltava views, are among the best in the capital.

## 8 New Town Hall
**⬛ F5 ⬛ Karlovo náměstí 1**
**⬛ Tower: 10am–6pm Tue–Sun**
**⬛ nrpraha.cz ⬛**

In 1419, an anti-clerical mob led by Jan Želivský hurled the Catholic mayor and his councillors from a New Town Hall window in the first of Prague's defenestrations (p25). The Gothic tower was added a few years later; its viewing platform is open to the public. Crowds of locals gather at the tower's base most Saturdays to congratulate newlyweds married in the building's Gothic hall.

---

### MŮSTEK

The area at the bottom of Wenceslas Square takes its name from the "Little Bridge" that spanned the moat here in medieval times. Below the surface, at the top of the escalators descending to the train platform, you'll find the remains of that bridge, uncovered by workers building the metro.

**The Dancing House, nicknamed "Ginger and Fred"**

# 9 Jerusalem Synagogue

📍 G3 🏛 Jeruzalémská 7 🕐 9am–6pm Sun–Fri 🌐 synagogue.cz/en/jerusalem-synagogue

Built between 1896 and 1906, this is Prague's youngest synagogue and perhaps its most striking. Architect Wilhelm Stiassny blended Moorish revival and Art Nouveau styling throughout the exterior and interior, to stunning effect. Two towers flank the horseshoe arch on the coloured façade, while the interior is decorated with rich colours and grand chandeliers, which dangle above the 850-seat space below.

# 10 Palackého náměstí

📍 E6

The riverside square is named for the 19th-century historian František Palacký, whose work was integral to the National Revival. Stanislav Sucharda's sweeping monument to him stands at the plaza's northern end, while the modern steeples of the Emmaus Monastery (p61) rise from the eastern edge. The church grounds are also known as the Slavonic Monastery.

**František Palacký Monument on Palackého náměstí**

## A DAY IN NOVÉ MĚSTO

## Morning

Head to **Wenceslas Square** (p42) to begin the day's sightseeing. Start with the **National Museum** (p122) at the top of the square, if only to see the marble stairway, the Pantheon and the city views from the dome. Walk to **St Wenceslas's Statue** and the monument to the victims of Communist rule. Enjoy a bit of retail therapy as you stroll northwest to Můstek, then visit the **Museum of Communism** (p122), or peacefully stroll through the **Franciscan Garden** (p119). Then walk ten minutes west down stately Národní třída towards the river for lunch at **Café Louvre** (p124).

## Afternoon

A short walk to the river and north along its banks leads you to the **National Theatre** for a glimpse at its magnificent façade. Then follow the Vltava south. Modern art buffs should stop at **Galerie Mánes** (p122) on the way. Further south, pause at Jiráskovo náměstí to admire the iconic **Dancing House**. Then turn left and follow Resslova uphill to the **Cathedral of Sts Cyril and Methodius** (p119).

Take in a performance at the National Theatre in the evening; **U Fleků** (p124) is the obvious choice for dinner. Then, head to **Radost FX** (p123) to dance the night away or to **Rocky O'Reilly's** (p123) for its cosy atmosphere and live music.

# Galleries and Museums

### 1. Galerie Mánes
🅿 E5 🏛 Masarykovo nábřeží 250
🕐 Hours vary, check website
🌐 ncvu.eu 🔗
Occupying the southern tip of Žofín Island, this contemporary art gallery hosts both Czech and foreign artists.

### 2. Galerie Via Art
🅿 E6 🏛 Resslova 6 🕐 1–5pm Mon–Fri
🌐 galerieviaart.com
Founded in 1991 as one of Prague's first private galleries, Galerie Via Art exhibits contemporary painting, sculpture and mixed-media art.

### 3. Lego Museum
🅿 L6 🏛 Národní 31 🕐 10am–8pm
daily 🌐 muzeumlega.cz
This Lego Museum is among the largest in the world. It may essentially be a gift shop with a museum attached, but the impressive Lego sculptures and interactive models will keep the kids entertained.

### 4. Mucha Museum
🅿 P5 🏛 Panská 7 🕐 10am–6pm daily
🌐 mucha.cz 🔗
Art Nouveau artist Alfons Mucha is a celebrated figure in the country. Here you'll find his journals, sketch-books and paintings, both private and commercial.

### 5. Museum of Senses
🅿 P5 🏛 Jindřišská 20 🕐 10am–10pm
daily 🌐 muzeumsmyslu.cz
This interactive museum has over 50 fun and engaging exhibits, including incredible optical illusions.

### 6. Museum of Communism
🅿 P3 🏛 V Celnici 4 🕐 9am–8pm daily
🌐 muzeumkomunismu.cz 🔗
A triptych of the dream, reality and nightmare that was Communist Czechoslovakia. The museum is filled with mementos.

### 7. Václav Špála Gallery
🅿 L6 🏛 Národní 30 🕐 11am–7pm daily 🌐 galerievaclava spaly.cz
This contemporary gallery exhibits works mainly by local artists and aims to make art more accessible.

### 8. National Museum
The collection across the two linked sites (p44) is mainly devoted to archaeology, anthropology, mineralogy, numismatics and natural history. But it also includes several excellent exhibitions on Prague and Czech history.

### 9. Police Museum
🅿 G7 🏛 Ke Karlovu 1 🕐 10am–5pm
Tue–Sun 🌐 muzeumpolicie.cz 🔗
Engaging exhibits, such as an interactive crime scene, document the history of the police in Prague.

### 10. Dvořák Museum
🅿 G6 🏛 Ke Karlovu 20 🕐 10am–5pm
Tue–Sun 🌐 nm.cz 🔗
This Baroque palace houses Antonín Dvořák's (p57) piano and viola, as well as other memorabilia.

**Stained glass, Mucha Museum**

Partygoers at Zone, a popular cocktail bar

# Nightspots

### 1. Radost FX
⌖ G6 ⌂ Bělehradshá 120 ☷ radostfx.cz
Late at night, club kids take over
the disco and lounge of this popular
club. Eclectic music is paired with
imaginative light shows, video pro-
jections, dancers and regular sets by
the best local and international DJs.

### 2. Balbi Bar
⌖ E4 ⌂ Mihulandshá 6 ☷ balbi
bar.com
Excellent cocktails, welcoming staff
and a cosy atmosphere make this bar
the perfect place to spend an evening.

### 3. Nebe Cocktail & Music Bar
⌖ G4 ⌂ Václavské náměstí 56
This bar has over 100 delicious
cocktails to choose from. Relax with
a drink under the vaulted ceilings,
or dance the night away to a mix of
current pop and R&B hits, as well
as music from the 1980s and 90s.

### 4. Lucerna Music Bar
⌖ N6 ⌂ Vodičkova 36 ☷ musicbar.cz
The granddaddy of Prague's clubs, the
cavernous Lucerna hosts concerts as
well as rock and dance parties.

### 5. Rocky O'Reilly's
⌖ F5 ⌂ Štěpánshá 32
☷ rockyoreillys.cz
Offering all a Celtophile could ask for,
this pub has live music in the evenings,
football on the TV, a roaring fire and
plenty of stout. The food here is decent.

### 6. Reduta Jazz Club
⌖ L6 ⌂ Národní 20 ☷ reduta
jazzclub.cz
Many celebrated musicians have
played here, as has former US
President Bill Clinton. Visit to
hear all types of jazz from swing
bands to modern styles.

### 7. Duplex Club
⌖ N6 ⌂ Václavské náměstí 21
During the day, Duplex is an ideal
location for lunch or dinner with good
views of the city. At night it turns into
one of Prague's most exclusive clubs.

### 8. Alcron Bar
⌖ G4 ⌂ Štěpánshá 40
Set in the luxurious Almanac X
Alcron hotel, this Art Deco-style
elegant bar offers a wide range
of unique signature cocktails,
drinks and delicious snacks.

### 9. Rock Café
⌖ L6 ⌂ Národní 20 ☷ rockcafe.cz
Conveniently set in the heart of the
city, Rock Café hosts live concerts
and has a multimedia space that
features a theatre and a gallery.

### 10. Zone
⌖ E5 ⌂ Křemencova 10 ☷ zonebar.cz
This atmospheric club in an original
stone cellar features stylish lighting
and a gracefully curvaceous long bar.
There's a separate lounge too, which
is a popular place for private events.

# Cafés and Pubs

**Art Nouveau interior of Kavárna Lucerna**

## 1. Kavárna Lucerna
📍 N6 🏠 Vodičkova 36 🌐 kavarna.lucerna.cz

This stylish "Lantern" café is the ideal place to enjoy coffee before watching a film or dancing at the nearby club.

## 2. La Casa de la Havana vieja
📍 E4 🏠 Opatovická 28 🌐 casahavana.cz

A classic Cuban cocktail bar, this spot captures the vibe of 1930s Cuba, offering a family-friendly atmosphere.

## 3. Café 35mm
📍 F5 🏠 Štěpánská 35

Students at the Institut Français and other Francophones gather here for coffee, quiche or a croissant.

## 4. Pilsnerka Národní
📍 E4 🏠 Národní 22 🌐 pilsnerkanarodni.cz

This is one of the best places to enjoy Pilsner Urquell. Try their tappings – milk, *šnyt* (cut) and *hladinka* (level).

## 5. Hospoda U Kalicha
📍 G6 🏠 Na bojišti 12–14 🌐 ukalicha.cz

This pub's decor and cartooned walls are based on the Czech novel *The Good Soldier Švejk*. Author Jaroslav Hašek (*p56*) set some of the pivotal scenes here.

## 6. Pivovarský dům
📍 F6 🏠 Ječná 16 🌐 pivo-dum.cz

A lovely restaurant and brewery, with traditional Czech interiors, which offers a unique range of beers.

## 7. Kavárna Adria
📍 M6 🏠 Národní 36

This café offers excellent coffee and homemade cakes.

## 8. Café Louvre
📍 L6 🏠 Národní 22 🌐 cafelouvre.cz

Franz Kafka, Max Brod and their writer friends used to hold court here. It's a bright, cheerful place, good for conversation and grabbing a bite to eat.

## 9. U Fleků
📍 E5 🏠 Křemencova 11 🌐 en.ufleku.cz

U Fleků is the city's oldest brewing pub, dating to 1499, and probably the most popular, and the reasonable prices reflect it. It is known for its dark lager.

## 10. Oliver's Coffee Cup
📍 G4 🏠 Václavské náměstí 58 🌐 oliverscoffeecup.cz

Named after the founder's sons, both called Oliver, this cosy café offers a variety of caffeinated drinks, all served by polite and attentive staff.

**U Fleků, Prague's famous beer hall**

# Restaurants

## 1. U Zpěváčků

📍 E5 ⌂ Na Struze 7
🌐 uzpevacku.com · ⓀⓀ

Established in 1865, this restaurant
is known for its beer and homemade
Czech cuisine.

## 2. Restaurace Bredovský dvůr

📍 P6 ⌂ Politichých vězňů 13
🌐 restauracebredovskyhydvur.cz · ⓀⓀ

Enjoy traditional Czech dishes such as
game goulash with Carlsbad dumplings.
In the summer, you can eat alfresco.

## 3. Namaste India Palackého

📍 F4 ⌂ Palackého 15 🌐 namaste
india.cz · ⓀⓀ

Come here for tasty, traditional Indian
cuisine. The restaurant offers an all-
you-can-eat buffet.

## 4. Čestr

📍 G4 ⌂ Legerova 75 🌐 cestr.
ambi.cz · ⓀⓀⓀ

Meat lovers will get a real kick out of
this top-notch smokehouse restaurant,
where cuts of beef and pork are cooked
to perfection.

## 5. U Pinkasů

📍 M6 ⌂ Jungmannovo náměstí 16
📞 221 111152 · ⓀⓀ

A great-value Czech beer hall since
1843, this is a very popular lunchtime
destination. Food is simple but hearty.

## 6. Modrý Zub

📍 N6 ⌂ Jindřišshá 5 🌐 modryzub.
com · ⓀⓀ

This is fast Thai food at its best, great
for a quick snack or light meal. Huge

**Old-fashioned Czech
pub-restaurant U Šumavy**

windows create a great opportunity
for people watching.

## 7. Lemon Leaf

📍 E5 ⌂ Myslíhova 14 🌐 lemon.cz · ⓀⓀ
There's a wide array of Thai and
Continental dishes. The ingredients
used are fresh, the presentation colour-
ful and service is fast and friendly.

## 8. Jáma³ Garden Pub

📍 F4 ⌂ V jámě 7 🌐 jamagarden
pub.cz · ⓀⓀ

Delicious Tex-Mex and American
specialities and a fun atmosphere.
Jáma organizes regular parties
and sports events.

## 9. U Šumavy

📍 E5 ⌂ Štěpánshá 3
🌐 usumavy.cz · ⓀⓀ

This old-fashioned pub restaurant
is a little piece of the Czech country-
side in central Prague. The food
is traditional – most meals are
served with dumplings.

## 10. Žofin Garden

📍 E5 ⌂ Slovanský ostrov 8
🌐 zofinrestaurant.cz · ⓀⓀⓀ

Near the National Theatre
on Slav Island, this restaurant
serves elevated takes on tradi-
tional Czech game dishes at
reasonable prices.

# GREATER PRAGUE

Prague's city centre can keep most visitors occupied for days, but if you're staying outside the city's heart, or if you have the time to explore beyond the capital's walls, the outlying areas offer plenty of surprises. Over the centuries, the various rulers of Prague have used the surrounding countryside as their personal playground, building impressive castles, palaces and parks to which they could escape the often claustrophobic streets and winding alleyways of the city. Even the Communists have left their own kind of functional mark on the area, with useful edifices, towers and exhibition spaces. From the peaceful parklands of Vyšehrad and the social atmosphere of Letná, to the noisy nightlife of Žižkov and the intriguing gardens of Holešovice and Troja, Greater Prague has a diversity that will fulfil almost any requirements you might have.

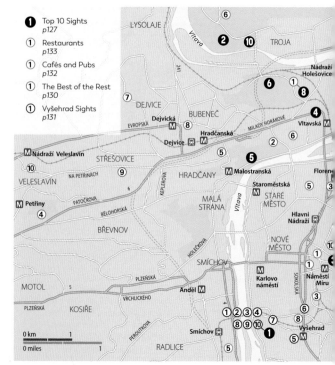

1 Top 10 Sights
p127

1 Restaurants
p133

1 Cafés and Pubs
p132

1 The Best of the Rest
p130

1 Vyšehrad Sights
p131

Historic Vyšehrad complex above the Vltava river

# 1 Vyšehrad
**Q R3**

The former fortress of Vyšehrad is steeped in legend. Bedřich Smetana paid tribute to the second seat of the Přemyslid dynasty that resided here in the 10th century in his opera *Libuše* and in his rousing work *Má vlast (p57)*. He is buried here in the National Cemetery, which is also home to the Slavín Monument *(p131)*.

# 2 Prague Zoo
**Q R1 Q U Trojského zámku 3, Troja Q Hours vary, chech website W zoopraha.cz**

This zoo is the second most popular attraction in the country after Prague Castle. Spread across a vast area, it is home to numerous bird and animal species, including elephants, gorillas and giant salamanders.

# 3 Vinohrady
**Q S2**

Originally the royal vineyards, Vinohrady today is a gently rolling residential neighbourhood. The central square, Náměstí Míru, features the Neo-Gothic Church of St Ludmila and the Art Nouveau Vinohrady Theatre. For a bit of peace and greenery, visit Havlíčkovy sady.

# 4 Holešovice
**Q R1**

Home to the National Gallery's Trade Fair Palace *(p54)*, which holds the gallery's collection of modern and contemporary art, this once-bustling warehouse district is being redeveloped to make a comeback. Motorcar enthusiasts will love the National Technical Museum *(p55)*, with its exhibits of Czech interwar vehicles such as Škodas, as well as other vintage vehicles.

## 5 Letná Park
📍 E1

A grand staircase leads from the Vltava riverbank opposite the Josefov quarter (p112) to a giant metronome. Prior to this oversized timekeeper, a mammoth stone statue of Joseph Stalin stood on the plinth here, but it was blown up in 1962. The surrounding wooded park echoes with the clatter of skateboards and barking dogs. Travelling circuses sometimes set up in the open fields, but Letná's biggest draw is probably its popular beer garden, which is found at the garden's eastern end.

## 6 Stromovka
📍 R1

King Ottokar II established the royal game park here in the 13th century; it's been a public garden since 1804 (stromovka means "place of trees"). Stroll or skate through the ancient park (p67) by day and visit the planetarium by night. The fish ponds were a creation of Rudolf II – the emperor drilled a tunnel under Letná in the 16th century to bring in water to supply them.

## 7 Žižkov TV Tower
📍 S2 📍 Mahlerovy sady 1
🕐 9am–midnight 🌐 towerparh.cz 📍

The Prague TV Tower is the highest building in Prague, reaching 216 m (709 ft) in height. However it didn't begin transmitting until after the Velvet Revolution (p11). Three thematically different "capsules" at the tower offer unforgettable views of the city, especially at sunset. Outside the tower, there are ten giant sculptures of babies by Czech artist David Černý.

## 8 Výstaviště
📍 R1

Originally built at the end of the 19th century to host trade shows, this exhibition ground is like nothing else in Prague. Although large parts of the complex are currently being renovated, including the Křižík fountain and the Lapidárium (p130), the area is still worth a visit on a rainy day for the country's largest aquarium, Mořský Svět. There's also an indoor swimming pool and an ice-hockey rink. The exterior of the Art Nouveau-style Industrial Palace is also a sight to behold.

---

### ŽIŽKOV

This neighbourhood came into existence when the city founders divided the Královské Vinohrady district. The inhabitants of the area thumbed their noses at Habsburg rule and named their new district after the Hussite warrior. Žižkovites' contrary nature runs deep, even having a separatist movement which promotes an independent Republic of Žižkov. An alternative culture thrives around the Akropolis club and the Divus artists collective.

Enjoying drinks in
Letná's beer garden

## 9 National Memorial on the Vítkov Hill

S2 Žižkov 10am–6pm
Wed–Sun nm.cz

The one-eyed Hussite general
Jan Žižka defeated invading
crusaders in 1420 atop the hill
where his giant equestrian statue
now stands in front of the Tomb
of the Unknown Soldier. Erected
in 1929, the monument serves as
a memorial to all those who
suffered in the Czech struggle
for independence. The Communists
co-opted the building, and for a
time it served as President Klement
Gottwald's mausoleum.

## 10 Troja Château

R1 U Trojského
zámku 1, Troja Apr–Oct:
10am–6pm Tue–Thu, Sat &
Sun; 1–6pm Fri ghmp.cz

One of the most striking
summer palaces in Prague,
Troja Château was built in the
late 17th century by Jean-Baptiste
Mathey for Count Sternberg. Sur-
rounded by beautiful gardens and
two orangeries, the château has
a good collection of 19th-century
art and sculpture.

Troja Château surrounded
by pretty gardens

## THREE AFTERNOON WALKS

### Afternoon One

See **Vyšehrad** (p127) late in the
day, but only if the weather looks
promising. Take the metro to the
Vyšehrad stop at the **Congress
Centre** (p131), from where you have
marvellous views of Prague's spires.
Walk west along Na Bučance and
enter the fortifications through
the **Tábor Gate** (p131). Once
inside the walls, you'll find historic
constructions everywhere, such
as the lovely Romanesque
**Rotunda of St Martin** (p131).
Enjoy the park at your leisure but
get to the westernmost edge of
the compound atop Vyšehrad's
rocky outcrop in time for sunset.

### Afternoon Two

**Žižkov** and **Vinohrady** (p127) are
also best seen in the second half
of the day. From Florenc metro,
climb to the **National Memorial
on the Vítkov Hill** for a wonderful
view, then compare it to the one
you get from the **Žižkov TV
Tower**. Take a stroll as far into
Vinohrady as your feet will permit
you, but save your strength: you'll
need it for a night out clubbing.

### Afternoon Three

Energetic and keen walkers can
manage to see **Stromovka** and
**Troja** in half a day. Take the tram
to **Výstaviště**, before crossing
the Vltava to the **Troja Château**.
From there, you're within easy
walking distance of **Prague Zoo**
(p127). Take bus 112 back to the
metro at Nádraží Holešovice.

# The Best of the Rest

### 1. Lapidárium
🅿 B5 🏛 Výstaviště 422, Holešovice
🕐 For renovation 🌐 nm.cz ♿
Several statues including the Marian column from Old Town Square (p28) and sculptures from Charles Bridge (p32) are on display here.

### 2. National Museum of Agriculture
🅿 B5 🏛 Kostelní 44, Holešovice
🕐 9am–5pm Tue–Sun 🌐 nzm.cz ♿
A visit to this museum is an excursion through Czech agricultural history.

### 3. The City of Prague Museum
🅿 H2 🏛 Na Poříčí 52 🕐 9am–6pm Tue–Sun 🌐 en.muzeumprahy.cz ♿
Visitors can explore the history of Prague at this museum.

### 4. Břevnov Monastery
🅿 Q2 🏛 Marhétská 1, Břevnov 🕐 Hours vary, chech website 🌐 brevnov.cz ♿
St Adalbert founded this Benedictine monastery in 993. You can see the remains of a Romanesque, 18th-century church

**Baroque Břevnov Monastery complex**

### 5. Bílek Villa
🅿 D1 🏛 Michiewiczova 1, Hradčany
🕐 10am–6pm Tue–Sun 🌐 ghmp.cz ♿
The exhibition of art at this villa captures the essence and style of František Bílek's body of work and techniques.

### 6. Olšany Cemetery
🅿 S2 🏛 Vinohradská 153 🕐 Mar, Apr, Oct: 8am–6pm daily; May–Sep 8am–7pm daily; Nov–Feb: 8am–5pm daily
Many notable Czech personalities, such as Jan Palach (p43) are buried in this vast cemetery. Visitors can get a free map at the entrance.

### 7. Kafka's Grave
🅿 C6 🏛 Izraelská 1 🕐 9am–5pm Sun–Tue, 9am–2pm Fri
Kafka's sombre gravemarker lies close to the entrance along Row 21 at the New Jewish Cemetery.

### 8. Church of the Most Sacred Heart of Our Lord
🅿 C6 🏛 Náměstí Jiřího z Poděbrad, Vinohrady
Designed by famous Slovenian architect Josip Plečnik, this modern building was inspired by old Christian architecture. Its most striking feature is the glass clock in the high tower wall.

### 9. Villa Müller
🅿 Q2 🏛 Nad Hradním vodojemem 14 🌐 muzeumprahy.cz/en/visit-villa-muller ♿
An avant-garde masterpiece, this villa by Adolf Loos is a fusion of Functionalism and old English-style design. Reservations needed.

### 10. DOX Centre for Contemporary Art
🅿 S1 🏛 Poupětova 1, Holešovice
🕐 Noon–6pm Wed–Sun 🌐 dox.cz ♿
Set in a former factory, this space presents contemporary international art, architecture and design.

# Vyšehrad Sights

**The Romanesque Rotunda of St Martin**

### 1. Sts Peter and Paul Cathedral

⬛ Štulcova ⬛ Apr–Oct: 10am–6pm daily (Nov–Mar: to 5pm) ↗

Although the first church to stand on this site was founded by Vratislav II in the 11th century, the Neo-Gothic structure seen today dates back to 1903.

### 2. Slavín Monument

⬛ K Rotundě ⬛ Mar, Apr, Oct: 8am–6pm daily (May–Sep: to 7pm; Nov–Feb: to 5pm)

Set within Vyšehrad Cemetery, this monument marks the burial place of a number of notable Czech cultural figures. Students laid flowers in remembrance here on 17 November 1989, before marching into town for the Velvet Revolution (p11).

### 3. Devil's Pillar

⬛ K Rotundě

The story goes that the devil bet a local priest that he could carry this pillar from the Church of St Mary in Prague to the boundaries of Rome before the clergyman could finish his sermon. Being a sore loser, Satan threw the column he was carrying to the ground here.

### 4. Tábor Gate (Špička)

⬛ V Pevnosti

Charles IV restored Vyšehrad's fortifications in the 14th century.

Catholic crusaders rode through this gate on their way to crush the Táborites in 1434.

### 5. Congress Centre

This ex-Communist palace of culture now hosts numerous international conferences as well as pop concerts, thanks to its excellent acoustics.

### 6. Nusle Bridge

This simple, utilitarian viaduct spans the Nusle Valley, connecting Nové Město to the Pankrác banking and commercial district.

### 7. Cubist Houses

Czech architect Josef Chochol (1880–1956) built several angular masterpieces in the early 20th century. Take the steps down the hill from Vyšehrad Cemetery to visit the impressive buildings at Rašínovo nábřeží 47, Libušina 49 and Neklanova 98.

### 8. Smetana's Grave

At the start of each year's Prague Spring International Music Festival (p84), musicians attend a ceremony at composer Bedřich Smetana's grave.

### 9. Casemates

⬛ V Pevnosti 46 ☎ 241 410348 ⬛ 10am–6pm daily ↗

In the 18th century, occupying French troops drilled niches in Vyšehrad rock and built vaults inside to store arms and ammunition. This now houses six original statues from Charles Bridge (p32).

### 10. Rotunda of St Martin

⬛ K Rotundě

This 11th-century chapel is the oldest in Prague and most likely to be the oldest Christian house of worship in the country. It was reconstructed in 1878.

# Cafés and Pubs

**Wood-panelled interior
of Pastička gastropub**

### 1. Kavárna Pražírna

🅖 G6 🏠 Lublaňská 676/50, Vinohrady
🅦 kavarnaprazirna.cz

Enjoy the flavour and aroma of freshly
roasted Arabica coffees at this café.

### 2. U Vystřeleného Oka

🅖 C6 🏠 U Božích bojovníků 3, Žižkov
🅒 222 540465 🅢 Sun

The name "At the Shot-Out Eye"
is a tribute to the half-blind Hussite
general Jan Žižka from whom Žižkov
takes its name and whose enormous
statue (p129) looms overhead.

### 3. U Holanů

🅖 H7 🏠 Londýnská 10, Vinohrady
🅦 uholanu.cz

Tuck into a plate of pickled sausages
or herring at Vinohrady's favourite
no-nonsense pub. Simple but clean,
with perfunctory service.

### 4. U Houdků

🅖 C6 🏠 Bořivojova 110, Žižkov
🅦 uhoudku.com

This hidden little gem in Žižkov serves
Czech meals that are great value for
money. In summer you can sit outside.

### 5. Palác Akropolis

🅖 C6 🏠 Kubelíkova 27, Žižkov
🅦 palacakropolis.com

One of the most active independent
cultural centres in Prague, Akropolis
annually hosts nearly 1,000 cultural
events. Both local as well as top
international artists perform here.

### 6. Café Letka

🅖 B5 🏠 Letohradská 44, Bubeneč
🅦 cafeletha.cz

With its social media-worthy good
looks, this café makes a delightful
stop at any time of day. Visit for brunch,
an afternoon coffee and cake or an
evening beer brewed by Matuška,
a brewer from Broum.

### 7. Dva Kohouti

🅖 B5 🏠 Sokolovská 55, Karlín
🅦 dvakohouti.cz

With dozens of beers on tap, this
brewery with a pub is a hugely popular
Karlín hangout. Try the exceptional
homebrewed pilsner.

### 8. Čep a pec

🅖 G6 🏠 Svatoplukova 528, Nusle
A friendly, family-run business that
prides itself on its authentic and
imaginative style. On offer is a wide
range of beers and freshly baked
goods. Refreshments are made from
produce supplied by local farmers.

### 9. Můj šálek kávy

🅖 B5 🏠 Křižíkova 105, Karlín
🅦 mujsalekkavy.cz

Sip away at speciality coffee and
savour homemade cakes and cookies
at the flagship café of Czech double-
shot coffee roasters. The interesting
decor includes bare walls, books
and artworks.

### 10. Pastička

🅖 B6 🏠 Blanická 25, Vinohrady
🅦 restaurace-pasticka.cz

The Mousetrap is a perfect blend
of old-fashioned beer hall and
modish gastropub. Visit it for a
choice of light and semi-dark
Bernard beer, good, filling food
and eclectic Irish decor.

# Restaurants

## 1. Aromi
**📍** H5 **🏠** Náměstí Míru 6, Prague 2
**🌐** aromi.lacollezione.cz · Ⓚ Ⓚ Ⓚ
This Italian restaurant serves up a menu of traditional food accompanied by wines from all around the world.

## 2. Olympos
**📍** C6 **🏠** Kubelíhova 9, Žižhov
**🌐** tavernaolympos.eu · Ⓚ Ⓚ
Prague's best Greek food is on offer here. The large garden, complete with a children's playground, is ideal for summer dining. The mixed salad platter is the best value around.

## 3. Mailsi
**📍** C6 **🏠** Lipanshá 1, Žižhov
**🌐** mailsi.cz · Ⓚ Ⓚ
This little Pakistani food spot is known for its simple interiors and good-value, flavourful food.

## 4. SaSaZu
**📍** C5 **🏠** Bubenské nábřeží 306, Holešovice **🌐** sasazu.com · Ⓚ Ⓚ Ⓚ
This Holešovice landmark offers a menu of exceptional dishes inspired by Asian street food. At night, it also becomes a popular live music venue.

## 5. Na Kopci
**📍** B6 **🏠** K Závěrce 20, Praha 5
**🌐** nakopci.com · Ⓚ Ⓚ Ⓚ
Featured in the Michelin guide as a "Bib Gourmand" restaurant, Na Kopci offers a four-course degustation menu of French and Czech delicacies created with seasonal and local ingredients.

## 6. Salabka
**📍** B5 **🏠** K Bohnicím 2, Praha 7
**🔒** Sun–Tue **🌐** salabka.cz · Ⓚ Ⓚ Ⓚ
Surrounded by vast vineyards, this restaurant, located near the district of Troja, is renowned for its award-winning wines. The menu here follows the latest

trends with wild game and offers local freshwater fish dishes.

## 7. Chorvatský Mlýn
**📍** A5 **🏠** Horoměřichá 3a, Praha 6, Dejvice **🌐** chorvatshymlyn.cz · Ⓚ Ⓚ Ⓚ
Standing on the site of the original 17th-century mill, "Croatian Mill" is located in the centre of the Divoká Šárka Nature Reserve.

## 8. U Cedru
**📍** B5 **🏠** Národní Obrany 27, Dejvice
**🌐** ucedru.cz · Ⓚ Ⓚ
For a traditional Lebanese dining experience, order pitta with hummus, tabbouleh and other appetizers.

## 9. ESKA
**📍** C6 **🏠** Pernerova 49, Karlín
**🌐** eska.ambi.cz · Ⓚ Ⓚ
Housed in a former fabric factory, this café, also a bakery and restaurant, serves breakfasts until late afternoon.

## 10. U Marčanů
**📍** A6 **🏠** Veleslavínshá 14, Prague 6
**🌐** umarcanu.cz · Ⓚ
Folk music and dancing make this a fun lunch spot. Large portions of Czech food are served at communal tables. Book ahead and take a taxi.

**Aromi's elegant dining room**

# STREETSMART

| | |
|---|---|
| Getting Around | 136 |
| Practical Information | 140 |
| Places to Stay | 144 |
| Index | 148 |
| Phrase Book | 156 |
| Acknowledgments | 158 |

*One of Prague's trams*

# GETTING AROUND

Whether exploring Prague by foot or making use of public transport, here is everything you need to know to navigate the city and the areas beyond the centre like a pro.

**AT A GLANCE**

**PUBLIC TRANSPORT COSTS**

SHORT TRIP

**Kč30**

30 mins
including transfers

SINGLE

**Kč40**

(zones 1–3)

DAY TICKET

**Kč120**

24 Hours
Unlimited travel

**NATIONAL SPEED LIMITS**

MOTORWAY

**130**
km/h
(80 mph)

EXPRESSWAYS

**110**
km/h
(70 mph)

NATIONAL ROADS

**90**
km/h
(60 mph)

URBAN AREAS

**50**
km/h
(30 mph)

## Arriving by Air

More than 60 international airlines fly to **Václav Havel Airport Prague** (PRG), situated 15 km (9 miles) northwest of the city centre in Ruzyně.

The airport has three terminals. Terminal 1 is used for intercontinental flights to the UK, North America, the Middle East, Africa and Asia. All domestic flights and flights to destinations within the EU and other Schengen countries are served by Terminal 2. These two terminals are connected and are only a short walk apart. Terminal 3, is used for general aviation and private planes.

Getting to and from Prague airport is easy, relatively fast and economical. Allow at least 60 minutes to reach the airport by road from the city centre at rush hour. Travelling by a combination of the metro and standard bus takes about 45 minutes depending on connections. There is a shared shuttle bus run by **Prague Airport Shuttles** that goes to the city centre every 15 minutes. You can also request to be dropped off at your accommodation. For information on journey times and ticket prices, see the table below.
**Václav Havel Airport Prague**
W prg.aero
**Prague Airport Shuttles**
W prague-airport-shuttle.cz

## International Train Travel

Regular high-speed international trains connect Prague's Hlavní nádraží and Nádraží Holešovice stations to major cities in Europe. Reservations for these services are essential as seats book up, particularly in the busy summer months.

You can buy tickets and passes for multiple international journeys from **Eurail** or **Interrail**, however you may still need to pay an additional reservation fee depending on what rail service you travel with. Always check that your pass is valid before boarding. Students and those under the age of 26 can benefit from discounted rail travel.

**Eurail**
W eurail.com
**Interrail**
W interrail.eu

## Domestic Train Travel

The railways in the Czech Republic are run by České Dráhy (**ČD**).

The biggest and busiest railway station in Prague is Hlavní nádraží, which is only a five-minute walk from Wenceslas Square. After a thorough renovation, the Art Nouveau station now features a gleaming interior with shops, restaurants, a pub and even a jeweller. The lower ground floor has an inexpensive left-luggage facility and the central ticket office (open 3:20am –12:30am). There is also a ČD Travel office, where all international rail tickets are available from multilingual station staff and ticket machines.

There are several types of train services operating in Prague and throughout the Czech Republic, including the *rychlík* (express) trains, which are used for longer distances; and the *osobní* (passenger) trains which form a local service and stop at all stations.

Tickets can be bought in advance. If you want to buy a ticket just before your train leaves, be aware that queues at ticket booths can be long.

On the timetable, an "R" in a box by a train number means you must have a seat reserved on that train. An "R" without a box means a reservation is recommended. If you are caught in the wrong carriage, you will have to pay an on-the-spot fine.
**ČD**
W cd.cz

## Public Transport

Prague's bus, tram and metro services are provided by the Prague Public Transport Company (**DPP**). Its website and app provide timetables, ticket information, transport maps and more.

The best way of getting around Prague by public transport is by tram or metro. Prague's rush hours are between 6am and 9am and 3pm and 5pm, Monday to Friday. However, more trains, trams and buses run at these times, so crowding is not usually a problem. Some bus routes to the suburbs only run during peak hours.
**DPP**
W dpp.cz

### Tickets

Prague has a fully integrated public transport system and tickets are valid on most forms of public transport. A separate ticket is needed for the funicular railway that runs from Újezd to the top of Petřín Hill.

Tickets are available from machines at metro stations, main tram stops and at most news stands (*tabák*).

Buy tickets before you travel and validate them in the machines provided. Periodic checks are carried out by ticket inspectors who will levy an on-the-spot fine if you are caught without a valid ticket. Those under six and over 70 travel free and tickets for people aged 6–15 and 60–65 years are half price (any form of ID card or passport is accepted).

Individual ticket prices add up; longer-term tickets are good value if you are planning on exploring the city thoroughly. Network tickets offer unlimited travel for for one day (Kč120) and three days (Kč330).

## GETTING TO AND FROM THE AIRPORT

| Transport | Journey time | Price |
| --- | --- | --- |
| Airport Express Bus | 35–50 mins | Kč60 |
| Metro/Bus/Night Bus | 45–50 mins | Kč32 |
| Shuttle Bus | 30 mins–1hr | Kč290 |
| Taxi | 30 mins–1hr | Kč600 |

## Buses

Visitors are likely to use a bus only to travel to and from the airport, or to sights further out of town. There are three bus lines that operate in Malá Strana, Staré Město and Nové Město.

Bus timetables are located at every stop. Daytime buses run from 5am to midnight every 6–30 minutes. Night buses (routes 901–915) operate from midnight to 4:30am and run every 20–60 minutes.

Validate your pre-bought tickets in the machine located at each door.

## Long-Distance Bus Travel

Long-distance bus or coach travel can be a cheap option for those visiting Prague. Some Czech towns, such as Karlovy Vary, Hradec Králové, Český Krumlov and Terezín, are much easier to reach by coach than train.

The city's main bus terminal is Florenc, on the northeastern edge of the Nové Město.

**Flixbus** and **RegioJet** offer a variety of routes to Prague from other European cities as well as several domestic routes.

**Flixbus**
ⓦ flixbus.com
**RegioJet**
ⓦ regiojet.com

## Trams

Prague's most efficient method of public transport is the city's comprehensive tram network, which covers a large area, including the city centre.

Maps and timetables at tram stops help you locate your destination and route. On the timetable, the stop you are at will be underlined and the direction of travel is given by the terminus station.

Routes 6, 9, 17 and 22 are the most useful for getting around the centre of Prague. They pass many of the major sights on both sides of the Vltava, and are a pleasant way of sightseeing.

Trams run 4:30am–12:30am daily. Night trams (routes 91–99) run every 30 minutes and are marked by white numbers on a dark background at stops.

## Metro

The metro is the fastest way to get around the city. Prague's underground system has four lines (A, B, C and D) operating from 5am until midnight.

Line A (green) is the most useful line for tourists, covering all the main areas of the city centre including the shopping area around Wenceslas Square.

Stations are signposted in both English and Czech, and feature information panels in a number of languages.

## Prague by Boat

Boat tours along the Vltava river offer fabulous views of Prague's major sights. Most run during the summer months, and include tours, romantic dinner cruises and private rentals.

Tickets can be booked in advance from tour providers. Check out **Evropská Vodní Doprava** or **Prague Boats**. Alternatively you can enquire on the day at the boarding points along the river.

**Prague Boats**
ⓦ prague-boats.cz
**Evropská Vodní Doprava**
ⓦ evd.cz

## Taxis

All taxis in Prague are privately owned, and there are many unscrupulous drivers who are out to charge as much as they can get away with. If you think you have been scammed by a taxi driver, take their name and number so you can report them to the police.

Look for Fair Place taxi ranks marked with a yellow "taxi" sign and an orange "thumbs up" icon. Taxis that stop here will guarantee the maximum charges of Kč40 boarding fee, Kč36 per km travel and Kč6 per minute waiting. After the journey, the driver is obliged to print an official receipt.

Taxi companies that are safe to hail on the street include **AAA Taxi**. However, the cheapest way to get a taxi is to phone or use the company's mobile app.

**AAA Taxi**
ⓦ aaataxi.cz

## Driving

Driving in Prague is not recommended. The city's complex web of one-way streets, lack of parking and pedestrianized areas make driving very difficult.

## Driving to Prague

The Czech Republic is easily reached by car from most countries in Europe via E-roads, the International European Road Network.

Prague is connected to every major border crossing by motorways (D roads. To drive on the motorway you will need to display a special highway toll sticker available at the border, petrol stations and post offices.

## Driving in Prague

Driving in Prague can be stressful and should be avoided. If you do drive, beware of cyclists and trams. Trams take precedence; take care when turning; and allow cyclists priority.

Vehicles must be parked on the right-hand side of the road, with the exception of one-way streets. Parking spaces in the centre are scarce, and the penalties for illegal parking are harsh. **Parkuj v klidu** provide detailed information regarding parking. Meter parking from 8am to 8pm costs a maximum Kč80 per hour and varies in price and length between orange, blue and violet zones. Unfortunately, car theft in Prague is rife. Try to park in an official – preferably underground – car park or at one of the guarded car parks (look for the "P+R" symbol) at the edge of the city and use public transport to travel into the centre.

If a car accident occurs, the vehicle cannot be moved until there has been a police inspection of the site. In case of emergency, you can call the road traffic assistance, Autoklub Bohemia Assistance (**ÚAMK**), by dialling the phone number 1240.

**Parkuj v klidu**
W parkujvklidu.cz

**ÚAMK**
W uamk.cz

## Car Rental

To rent a car in the Czech Republic, you must be at least 21 years old and have held a valid licence for at least one year. Drivers under the age of 26 may incur a young driver surcharge.

## Rules of the Road

Always drive on the right. Unless signposted otherwise, vehicles coming from the right have right of way.

At all times, drivers must carry a valid driver's licence, registration and insurance documents.

The law states that all occupants should wear seat belts. Small children must travel in the back seat and the use of a mobile phone while driving is strictly prohibited, with the exception of a hands-free system.

## Cycling

Prague is generally a bike-friendly city, with many cycle lanes. Bicycles can be rented hourly or by the day. Deposits are usually paid upfront and refunded on return. **Praha Bike** offers private rentals and tours while public bicycle schemes such as **Rekola**, operated through an app, are also available.

Ride on the right. Beware of tram tracks; cross them at an angle to avoid getting stuck. For your own safety, do not walk with your bike in a bike lane or cycle in pedestrian zones, or in the dark without lights. Wearing a helmet is recommended.

**Praha Bike**
W prahabike.cz

**Rekola**
W rekola.cz

## Walking

The city centre is compact and walking is the best way to see the city. Wear flat-soled comfortable shoes, watch your step on the cobblestones and be aware that trams have priority.

Guided walking tours abound, with themes that include historic Prague and haunted Prague. Most meet below the Astronomical Clock in Old Town Square.

# PRACTICAL INFORMATION

A little local know-how goes a long way in Prague. On these pages you can find all the essential advice and information you will need to make the most of your trip to this city.

## AT A GLANCE

**CURRENCY**
Czech Koruna (CZK)

**AVERAGE DAILY SPEND**

| SAVE | SPEND | SPLURGE |
|------|-------|---------|
| Kč2500 | Kč4000 | Kč5000+ |

| BOTTLED WATER | COFFEE | BEER | DINNER FOR TWO |
|---------------|--------|------|----------------|
| Kč25 | Kč65 | Kč45 | Kč1,250 |

## ESSENTIAL PHRASES

| Hello | Dobrý den |
|-------|-----------|
| Goodbye | Na shledanou |
| Please | Prosím |
| Thank you | Děkuji vám |
| Do you speak English? | Mluvíte anglicky? |
| I don't understand... | Nerozumím |

**ELECTRICITY SUPPLY**
Power sockets are type E, fitting two-pronged plugs. Standard voltage is 230 volts.

## Passports and Visas
For entry requirements, including visas, consult your nearest Czech embassy or check the **Ministry of Foreign Affairs of the Czech Republic** website. Citizens of the UK, US, Canada, Australia and New Zealand do not need a visa for stays of up to three months, but must apply in advance for the European Travel Information and Authorization System (**ETIAS**); roll-out has continually been postponed so check website for details. Visitors from other countries may also require an ETIAS, so check before travelling. EU nationals do not need a visa or an ETIAS.
**ETIAS**
🌐 etiasvisa.com
**Ministry of Foreign Affairs of the Czech Republic**
🌐 mzv.cz

## Government Advice
It is important to seek both your and the Czech government's advice before travelling. The **UK Foreign, Commonwealth & Development Office (FCDO)**, the **US State Department**, the **Australian Department of Foreign Affairs and Trade** and the Ministry of Foreign Affairs of the Czech Republic offer the latest information on security, health and local laws.
**Australian Department of Foreign Affairs and Trade**
🌐 smartraveller.gov.au
**FCDO**
🌐 gov.uk/foreign-travel-advice
**US State Department**
🌐 travel.state.gov

## Customs Information
You can find information on the laws relating to goods and currency taken in or out of the Czech Republic on the **Customs Administration of the Czech Republic** website.
**Customs Administration of the Czech Republic**
🌐 celnisprava.cz

## Insurance

We recommend taking out a comprehensive insurance policy covering theft, loss of belongings, medical care, cancellations and delays, and read the small print carefully. The Czech Republic has reciprocal health agreements with other EU countries. EU and UK citizens are eligible for free emergency treatment provided they have a valid European Health Insurance Card (EHIC) or UK Global Health Insurance Card (**GHIC**).

**GHIC**
W ghic.org.uk

## Vaccinations

No vaccinations are necessary.

## Money

Most establishments accept major credit, debit and prepaid currency cards. Contactless payments are becoming increasingly common, but it's always a good idea to carry some cash for smaller items and local markets.

Tipping in restaurants (around 10 per cent) is considered polite – though overzealous tipping can cause embarrassment. In hotels, porters generally expect Kč50 per bag, housekeeping Kč30 per day and the concierge Kč30–50 per day. Taxi drivers don't expect a tip.

## Travellers with Specific Requirements

Narrow streets and uneven paving make Prague difficult for wheelchair users. However, services are improving. Most public buildings are now fitted with entry ramps.

Most of the trams and buses have low access, and the majority of metro stations are fitted with lifts. Timetables at tram stops indicate which services are wheelchair-accessible. Visit the Prague Public Transport Company (**DPP**) website to plan your journey using wheelchair-accessible metro stations, trams and buses.

Airport assistance is available for free but must be booked in advance through your airline or travel agency. **Accessible Prague** can arrange transport from the airport to the city centre for wheelchair users. They can also help with finding suitable accommodation and they organize tours and day trips tailored to visitors' needs.

The **Prague Organization of Wheelchair Users** has a range of resources available, including interactive maps and guides in Braille.

**Accessible Prague**
W accessibleprague.com
**Prague Organization of Wheelchair Users**
W presbariery.cz
**Prague Public Transport Company**
W dpp.cz/en/barrier-free-travel

## Language

Czech is the official language of the Czech Republic. Those working in the tourist industry usually have a good level of English, but it's appreciated if you know a few phrases in Czech.

## Opening Hours

Shops in the city centre generally open from 9am to 6pm Monday to Saturday. Malls and shopping centres stay open until 8pm or 9pm. Some shops close early on Saturdays and close for the day on Sundays. Public transport also runs a reduced service at weekends.

Various museums and attractions are closed on Mondays. Last admission to many attractions is 30 minutes before closing.

On public holidays, schools, banks and most public services are closed and some museums, attractions and shops are closed while others will close early.

Situations can change quickly and unexpectedly. Always check before visiting attractions and hospitality venues for up-to-date opening hours and booking requirements.

## Personal Security

Prague is relatively safe and violence is rare. Pickpocketing is common, particularly on crowded trams and the metro, and at popular tourist sites. Use your common sense and be alert to your surroundings. Avoid hailing taxis on the street; instead, call or ask someone to call a reliable radio taxi *(p138)*.

If you have anything stolen, report the crime as soon as possible to the nearest police station, and bring ID with you. Get a copy of the crime report in order to claim on your insurance.

If you have your passport stolen, or if you are involved in a serious crime or accident, contact your embassy as soon as possible.

Generally, Czechs are accepting of all people, regardless of their race, gender or sexuality. Prague has an active LGBTQ+ scene with many venues for the community and an annual Pride event, held each August. Homosexuality was legalized in 1962 but same-sex marriages aren't recognized in Czech law. If you do feel unsafe, the **Safe Space Alliance** pinpoints your nearest place of refuge.

**Safe Space Alliance**
w safespacealliance.com

## Health

The Czech Republic has a world-class healthcare system. Emergency medical care is free for all UK and EU citizens. If you have an EHIC or GHIC *(p141)*, be sure to present this as soon as possible.

For other visitors, payment of hopsital bills and medical expenses is the patient's responsibility. As such it is important to arrange comprehensive medical insurance beforehand. You may still have to pay upfront for medical treatment and reclaim later.

For minor ailments and prescriptions go to a pharmacy *(lékárna)*. These are easily identified by a large green cross. Details of the nearest 24-hour service are usually displayed in windows.

## Smoking, Alcohol and Drugs

Prague has a strict smoking ban in all public spaces including buildings, bars, cafés, shops, restaurants and hotels.

The possession of narcotics is limited. Possession of illegal substances could result in prosecution and a possible prison sentence.

There is no blanket ban on the consumption of alcohol on the streets;

however, drinking alcohol on the bus or train and in metro stations, parks, playgrounds and near schools is banned and may incur a fine. Many Staré Město streets have banned walking around with an open bottle or can.

The Czech Republic enforces a strict zero tolerance policy on drink-driving. This also applies to cyclists.

## ID
It is compulsory for visitors to carry a form of ID at all times, or failing that, a photocopy of your passport.

## Responsible Tourism
As one of Europe's most-visited cities, Prague suffers from overtourism and inebriated visitors are a real problem. Do your bit to support the city by being considerate to locals, particularly in residential areas (making loud noises in some areas can incur a fine).

Returnable cups are common in markets and at events, so make use of them and avoid single-use plastics. Dropping litter on the streets and in parks comes with a hefty on-the-spot fine, so use publicly available bins or take your litter with you.

Buying local goes a long way; avoid tourist traps and seek out locally owned retailers and crafters.

## Visiting Places of Worship
Dress respectfully; talk quietly and avoid using flash photography. When visiting synagogues, cover your head and never turn your back on the ark.

## Mobile Phones and Wi-Fi
Free Wi-Fi hotspots are widely available in Prague's city centre. Cafés and restaurants usually permit the use of their Wi-Fi on the condition that you make a purchase. Visitors travelling to Prague with EU tariffs can use their devices abroad without being affected by data roaming charges. Users will be charged the same rates for data, SMS and voice calls as they would pay at home.

## Postal Services
Stamps can be bought from post offices, newsagents and tobacconists (tabák).

Parcels and registered letters must be sent from a post office. There is no first- or second-class mail, but the majority of letters usually arrive at their destination within a few days.

## Taxes and Refunds
VAT in the Czech Republic is usually around 20 per cent for most items. Non-EU residents are entitled to a tax refund on single purchases exceeding Kč2000, subject to certain conditions. This does not include tobacco or alcohol.

When you make a purchase, ask the sales assistant for a tax-free cheque. When leaving the country, present this form, along with the goods receipt and your ID at customs.

## Discount Cards
There are a number of passes or cards available to tourists visiting the city.

One such card is the **Prague Cool Pass**, which provides free entry to over 70 attractions and discounted entry to many more, as well as discounted tours, cruises and concerts. Passes are valid for one to ten days (from €55 to €139) and are available as a digital pass via a mobile app or as a physical card.

Free or discounted entry to Prague's most popular tours and attractions is included with **Prague City Pass**. The card costs Kč1390 and is valid for 30 days from first use. Available online and from participating tourist offices.

The **Prague Visitor Pass** includes entry to almost 70 attractions, discounts on tours, events and more, plus free travel on public transport. The card is valid for 48, 72 or 120 hours from first use and is available online and from some official Prague tourist offices.

**Prague City Pass**
ⓦ praguecitypass.com
**Prague CoolPass**
ⓦ praguecoolpass.com
**Prague Visitor Pass**
ⓦ praguevisitorpass.eu

# PLACES TO STAY

From opulent Art Nouveau hotels to cosy family-run inns, Prague has a hotel to suit every type of traveller. Seeking a luxurious stay? Bed down in a former palace. All about location? Choose a hotel next to the Charles Bridge or Old Town Square. Want to be in the thick of the nightlife scene? Go for a hostel in Greater Prague.

Historic hotels are everywhere, but take the chance to explore the city's quirkier side too, perhaps staying on a moored boat along the river or a retro spot with Pop Art flourishes.

**PRICE CATEGORIES**

For a standard, double room per night (with breakfast if included), taxes and extra charges.

**Kč** under Kč3,000
**Kč Kč** Kč3,000–6,000
**Kč Kč Kč** over Kč6,000

## Staré Město

### Ahoy! Hostel

**Q** L6 **⌂** Na Perštýně 10 **W** ahoyhostel.com · **Kč**

It's hard to find an excellent, low-cost option in Staré Město, but that's where Ahoy! comes in. With those pennies you've saved you can treat yourself to a cheap Czech beer from the hostel's fridge or explore the Old Town Square, just a five-minute walk away. Or, keep costs down even further at the hostel's free evening events.

### Aurus Hotel

**Q** K4 **⌂** Karlova 3 **W** adrezliving.com · **Kč Kč**

If you're seeking a peaceful getaway but still want to be in the thick of the action, book into the family-run Aurus Hotel. Though situated on the historic Royal Route, just minutes away from Charles Bridge and the Old Town Square, the UNESCO-listed building sits on the quietest street in the area. Inside, it's an old-world sanctuary, with rooms complemented by high-beamed ceilings, wooden fittings and antique furnishings.

### Hotel Josef

**Q** N2 **⌂** Rybná 20 **W** hoteljosef.com · **Kč Kč**

Hoping to keep up your fitness regime on holiday? Hotel Josef will keep you on track. Not only is this modern, minimalist hotel home to a superb rooftop gym, it also hosts free organized runs every Tuesday and Friday morning. Get your sweat on then enjoy a smoothie and freshly baked goods from the onsite French bakery.

### Buddha-Bar Hotel

**Q** N3 **⌂** Jakubská 649/8 **W** buddhabarhotel prague.com · **Kč Kč**

With its dragon murals, decadent red-and-gold colour scheme and a 3-ft (1-m) Buddha in the lobby, this luxury hotel is a slice of east Asia in central Europe. The theme extends to the amenities, too; the restaurant serves delicious pan-Asian dishes, and the spa offers signature rituals like the so-called "Journey to Bali".

### The Emblem Hotel

**Q** L3 **⌂** Platnéřská 19 **W** emblemprague.com · **Kč Kč Kč**

This five-star hotel is adored for many reasons: an excellent spa, a stunning collection of contemporary art and various chill-out spaces where both locals and visitors can lounge, drink or work. Above all, though, it's the George Prime Steak – one of the city's best steak restaurants – that people shout about the most; try the T-bone.

### Hotel Paříž

**Q** P3 **⌂** U Obecního domu 1 **W** hotel-paris.cz · **Kč Kč Kč**

With its vaulted ceilings, golden statues and grand lobby staircase, this hotel is a time capsule of early 20th-century Art Nouveau elegance. A complimentary drink at check-in is the cherry on top.

## The Mozart

**Ⓥ** K5 **Ⓐ** Karolíny Světlé 34
**Ⓦ** themozart.com · Kč Kč Kč

It's said that Count Jan Pachta, who owned this former palace, jokingly locked Mozart in one of the rooms here until he composed a piece for Pachta's orchestra. True or not, Mozart did indeed stay here in his heyday. Follow suit and you're promised a beautiful riverside location, sumptuous rooms and romantic courtyards that host summer concerts.

## Malá Strana

### Vintage Design Hotel Sax

**Ⓥ** B3 **Ⓐ** Jánský vršeh 3
**Ⓦ** sax.cz · Kč Kč

This retro hotel is worlds away from its neigh-bouring medieval mon-uments, and therein lies its unique charm. All rooms are decorated in styles that reflect the 50s, 60s and 70s, like abstract wallpaper and Pop Art touches, and decked out with original period furniture. It's a short walk to the Lennon Wall, should you desire more bohemian vibes.

### Hotel Pod Věží

**Ⓥ** D3 **Ⓐ** Mostecká 2
**Ⓦ** podvezi.com · Kč Kč

There's a novelty to staying right by the tower at Charles Bridge, but that's not all this hotel has going for it. Its creperie is the icing on the cake (or the topping on the crepe), serving up sweet and savoury crepes as well as fresh sandwiches and salads.

### Golden Well Hotel

**Ⓥ** C2 **Ⓐ** U Zlaté studně 4
**Ⓦ** goldenwell.cz · Kč Kč Kč

This place is worth a stay for the breakfast on the rooftop terrace alone. Luckily, there's plenty more to keep you happy here, starting with its romantic location in a 16th-century regal residence, set beside the adjoining Ledeburg Gardens. Better yet, rooms feature whirlpool baths and stunning Richelieu furniture.

### Charles Bridge Hostel

**Ⓥ** D3 **Ⓐ** Mostecká 4
**Ⓦ** charlesbridgehostel.com · Kč

As its name suggests, this hostel is all about location, location, location. Close to the Charles Bridge, it's a budget-friendly option in a fairly expensive part of the city, and your money goes even further here with the free tours, guidebook rentals and discounts on several experiences in Prague.

### The Augustine

**Ⓥ** D2 **Ⓐ** Letenshá 12/33
**Ⓦ** marriott.com · Kč Kč Kč

It might be part of the Marriott's "Luxury Collection" today, but this former 13th-century monastery hasn't forgotten its roots. Vaulted ceilings, original doors and exposed beams are a reminder of the complex's past life, and former monks' quarters have been transformed into beautiful rooms with decor inspired by 20th-century Czech Cubism. Oh, and the monastery still brews its own beer according to an Augustinian monastic recipe; enjoy a pint in the hotel's restaurant.

## Prague Castle and Hradčany

### Questenberg Hotel

**Ⓥ** A3 **Ⓐ** Úvoz 15/155
**Ⓦ** questenberg.cz · Kč Kč

Views, glorious views! Stay at this small Baroque hotel and you'll be treated to stunning vistas over Prague, from the Petřín Gardens down to Malá Strana and Staré Město. The price to pay for such a treat is a relatively long uphill walk from Malá Strana, but trust us when we say it's worth it.

### Romantický Hotel U Raka

**Ⓥ** A2 **Ⓐ** Černínská 10
**Ⓦ** hoteluraka.cz · Kč Kč

Everything about this family-run place feels suitably homely. On a quiet street near Prague Castle, 18th-century timber walls encase cosy, country-style rooms dotted with antique furnishings. When making a reservation, book room No 6, which has its own private garden and a fireplace. This is truly a lovely place to be.

## Hotel Savoy

**A2** **Keplerova 6**
**savoyprague.cz · Kč Kč**

What do Tina Turner, David Bowie and the Spice Girls have in common? Aside from their singing chops, they've all bedded down at this grand hotel, a former 19th-century cinema that retains its star quality today. The Art Nouveau building exudes historic glamour, with a marble-floored lobby, vintage furniture in the common areas and rooms decked out with traditional wooden furnishings and patterned carpets.

## Josefov and Northern Staré Město

### Residence Bene

**N2** **Dlouhá 48**
**residence-bene.cz · Kč**

Locations rarely get much better than this, let alone at this price. Book a stay here and you're just minutes from the best sites in both Josefov and Staré Město, including a quick hop, skip and jump to the Old Town Square. The rooms are no-frills, but you'll hardly be spending much time inside.

### River Hotel Königstein

**L1** **Königstein, Dvořákovo nábřeží**
**riverhotel.cz · Kč Kč**

Even better than taking a boat tour along the Vltava river? Letting its gentle waters lull you to sleep. This place offers something completely different from the rest of the city – the chance to stay on a moored boat on the river's banks. And when you wake, step onto the upper deck for breakfast with views of Prague Castle.

### The President

**L1** **Náměstí Curieových 1** **axxos hotels.com · Kč Kč Kč**

The Brutalist exterior of this former communist building couldn't be more different from its slick modern interior. Rooms are kitted out with designer furniture, beautiful artworks and huge windows that let in ample light – perfect for looking out across the river over to Prague Castle. Best of all, the excellent Elements restaurant serves top Czech and global cuisine.

## Nové Město

### MeetMe23

**G4** **Washingtonova 23** **meetme23.com · Kč**

Forever losing your room key? MeetMe23 has got your back; you unlock your room with your phone here, and that's just the start of how this hotel embraces tech. A virtual receptionist greets you when you arrive, a "virtual flight" video over Prague inspires your itinerary and there's even a 3D printer where you can print out a souvenir of the so-called "Blueman", a blue figure you'll see around the hotel. It's wacky, forward-thinking and, ironically, housed in a historic building.

### The ICON

**F4** **V jámě 6**
**iconhotel.eu · Kč Kč**

The ICON is proof that luxury can be found at a reasonable price. Rooms include high-end amenities you'd expect from truly luxurious places, including high thread-count bed linens that cover natural, handmade Swedish beds and complimentary Rituals toiletries. An excellent tapas restaurant and all-day breakfast top it off.

### Mosaic House Design Hotel

**E5** **Odboru 4**
**mosaichouse.com · Kč Kč**

Mosaic isn't just about offering you the best stay (but that it does, with cosy rooms, a stylish café and private spa). It's also committed to offering a sustainable stay. Not only was this the first hotel in the Czech Republic to reuse and recycle waste water, it was also the country's first $CO_2$-neutral hotel, and even makes its own soil. A beautiful garden oasis seals the deal.

### NYX Hotel Prague

**P5** **Panshá 9** **nyx-hotels.com/prague · Kč Kč**

If you want to feel like you're staying in a work of art, book into NYX.

This design-led hotel was originally designed by the famous Modernist architect Josef Gočár, and it's filled with street art by local artists that lend the space a sense of urban chic. Things gets even cooler at the 360° Lounge Bar, where signature cocktails are served to live music.

## Hotel NH Collection Prague Carlo IV

**H3** **Senovážné náměstí 13** **dahotels. com** · Kč Kč Kč

This hotel might be set in a former 19th-century palace, but it wasn't royalty who spent time here; rather, the building was a former bank, and you get what you pay for at this sophisticated spot. Choose a room in the "historical wing", filled with beautifully designed Italian furniture, and lean into the opulence at the bar, set in an old bank vault.

## Miss Sophie's New Town

**G6** **Melounova 3** **miss-sophies.com** · Kč

What makes this place so loved? It could be the spa, where you can relax in a hot tub, sweat it out in an infrared sauna and snack on nuts and fruit in between. Or maybe it's the buffet breakfast, a top display of meats, cheeses, omelettes and pancakes. Whatever it is, Miss Sophie's is the perfect retreat from the bustle of the city.

## The Grand Mark

**G3** **Hybernská 12** **grandmark.cz** · Kč Kč Kč

Nestled in a former Baroque palace, the Grand Mark is still fit for royalty today. Rooms are elegantly furnished, the Le Grill Restaurant serves up beautifully plated dishes beneath a grand chandelier, and a private courtyard garden is the ideal place to pass a peaceful evening.

## Greater Prague

## Czech Inn

**R2** **Francouzská 76, Vršovice** **czech-inn. com** · Kč

You're going to want to check in to this hostel – it could well be Prague's most sociable. Live music, DJs, movie nights and quizzes are just some of the events that keep guests entertained at night, all of which are the perfect way to meet people to explore the popular bars along nearby Krymská with.

## Brix Hostel

**S2** **Roháčova 15, Žižkov** **brixhostel. com** · Kč

You'll be hard-pressed to find somewhere more ideally located for Žižkov's vibrant nightlife scene. With a large communal terrace and multi-bed dorms (including all-female options), Brix is perfect for meeting likeminded night owls to hit the town with. And, if you're lucky, a stay at Brix

might even coincide with one of the hostel's impromptu party nights.

## Mama Shelter

**R1** **Veletržní 1502/20, Holešovice** **mama shelter.com/prague** · Kč Kč

The local branch of a trendy global chain, Mama Shelter is popular for good reason. An epic terrace for casual drinks? Check. A legendary Sunday brunch? Correct. Pool tables and table football? Naturally. Add to that DJ nights and you've got a hotel you'll struggle to leave.

## Botanique Hotel

**R2** **Sokolovská 11, Karlín** **hotelbotanique. com** · Kč Kč

The Botanique means business when it comes to eco-friendly practices. Recyclable Nespresso capsules feature in every room, keys are wooden (not plastic) and vegan and vegetarian menus are offered (online, to save paper). Even better, you can charge your electric car here for free.

## Hotel Le Palais

**R2** **U Zvonařky 1, Vinohrady** **lepalais hotel.eu** · Kč Kč Kč

If you're looking for a plush belle époque villa stay in one of Prague's most desirable neighbourhoods, Le Palais is for you. You'll have access to your own reading room, a spa and wellness centre. Step outside for the gorgeous Havlíčkovy sady park.

# INDEX

Page numbers in **bold** refer to main entries.

### A

Absinth 61
Accommodation
    budget tips 83
    places to stay 144–7
Air travel 136, 137
Alchemy 61
Alcohol 142–3
Altars of Sts Felicissimus
    and Marcia (Loreta) 35
Altdorfer, Albrecht,
    *Martyrdom of St Florian* 41
Antiques 101, 116
Apartments 83
Apocalypse Cycle (St Agnes
    of Bohemia Convent) 41
Arcade (Loreta) 35
Architecture 12
Art 57
    *see also* Museums and
    galleries
Art Deco (shop) 80, 92
Artěl 80–81, 101
Ashkenazi, Eliezer ben
    Elijah 39
Astronomical Clock 30, 31,
    82, 91
Auction houses 80

### B

Bars and pubs 74, 78–9
    budget tips 83
    Greater Prague 132
    Malá Strana 102
    Nové Město 124
    Prague Castle and
        Hradčany 108
    Staré Město 94
    *see also* Nightlife
Basilica of St James 50–51,
    73, 90, 91
Bassevi, Hendl 38
Beer 12, 61, 77, 83

Beer spas 74
Bel Art Gallery 101
Bell Tower (Loreta) 34
Beneš, Edvard 25
Bethlehem Square 91
Bicycle rental 139
Bílek Villa 130
Black Angel's 79, 93
Black Light Theatre 71
Boat trips 71, 75, 138
Bohemia International
    Folklore Dance Festival
    84–5
Bohemian Chancellery
    (Old Royal Palace) 24
Bohemian Crown Jewels
    (St Vitus Cathedral) 27
Book shops 101
Botanical Garden of Charles
    University 82
Botanical Garden Troja
    70–71
Botanicus 80, 92
Břevnov Monastery 130
Bruncvík 32–3
Budget tips 83
Buquoy Palace 100
Bus travel 83, 138

### C

Cabaret 74
Cafés 78–9
    Greater Prague 132
    Josefov and Northern
        Staré Město 117
    Malá Strana 102
    Nové Město 124
    Prague Castle and
        Hradčany 108
    Staré Město 94
Café Savoy 79, 103
Café Slavia 78, 94
Calvary (Charles Bridge) 32
Čapek, Karel 56, 57
Capuchin Cycle (St Agnes of
    Bohemia Convent) 41

Car rental 139
Casanova, Giacomo 98
Casemates (Vyšehrad) 131
Castles and fortifications
    Daliborka Tower (Prague
        Castle) 23
    Hunger Wall 47
    Prague Castle **22–5**, 105,
        107
    Prague's Walls and Gates
        91
    Tábor Gate (Vyšehrad)
        129, 131
    Vyšehrad Castle 52, 61,
        127
    White Tower (Prague
        Castle) 22
Cathedrals *see* Churches
    and cathedrals
Celetná 90, 91
Cellar bars 74
Celtic tribes 8
Cemeteries
    Old Jewish Cemetery 37,
        38, 82, 113, 115
    Olšany Cemetery 130
    Vyšehrad Cemetery 82
Ceremonial Hall (Jewish
    Museum) 36–7, 114
Černín Palace 107
Černý, David, Upside-Down
    Horse Statue 43, 68
Český Porcelán 92
Chapels *see* Churches and
    cathedrals
Charles Bridge **32–3**, 97,
    99
Charles IV 9, 25
Chochol, Josef 131
Christmas 85
Churches and cathedrals
    50–51
    Basilica of St James
        50–51, 73, 90, 91
    Cathedral of Sts Cyril and
        Methodius 51, 119, 121

Churches and cathedrals
(cont)
Chapel of All Saints (Old
Royal Palace) 24
Chapel of the Holy Cross
(Prague Castle) 23
Church of the Most
Sacred Heart of Our
Lord 130
Church of the Nativity
(Loreta) 35
Church of Our Lady
before Týn 28–9, 51
Church of Our Lady of the
Snows 43
Church of Our Lady
Victorious 50, 99
Church of St Lawrence 47
Church of Sts Simon and
Jude 73
etiquette 143
Gothic Chapel (Old Town
Hall) 30
Loreta 34–5, 50, 106, 107
Mirror Chapel
(Clementinum) 73, 90
music recitals 73
New Archbishop's Chapel
(St Vitus Cathedral) 27
Rotunda of St Martin
(Vyšehrad) 129, 131
Royal Oratory (St Vitus
Cathedral) 27
St Cajetan Church 73
St George's Basilica
(Prague Castle) 23, 73
St Martin in the Wall 73
St Nicholas Cathedral 29,
73, 91
St Nicholas Church Malá
Strana 50, 73, 98, 99
Sts Peter and Paul
Cathedral (Vyšehrad)
131
St Vitus Cathedral **26–7**,
50, 105, 107
Wenceslas Chapel (St
Vitus Cathedral) 27
*see also* Monasteries and
convents

City of Prague Museum
54–5, 130
Clementinum 73, 90, 91
Clubs 75
Nové Město 123
Staré Město 93
Cocktail bars 74
Coffee and cake 13
Cold War
Cold War Museum 43
Crisis Fallout Shelter
43
Folimanka Underground
Bunker 65
Communism 10, 11
Communist Memorial
42–3
monuments 13
Museum of Communism
121, 122
Congress Centre (Vyšehrad)
129, 131
Convents *see* Monasteries
and convents
Crime 142
Crisis Fallout Shelter 43
Crystal 80, 92, 101, 116
Cubism 68, 131
Culture 12
Currency 140
Customs information 140
Cycling 139
Czechoslovakia 10–11
Czech Republic 11
Czechs 61
Czech Statehood Day 85

**D**
Daliborka Tower (Prague
Castle) 23
Dance 72, 84–5
Dancing House 120, 121
Day of the Fight for
Freedom and Democracy
85
Day of Liberation 85
Defenestrations of Prague
9, 25
Delmedigo, Joseph
Solomon 39

Demonstrations, historic
43
Devil's Pillar (Vyšehrad) 131
Diet (Old Royal Palace) 24
DinoPark 70
Disabled travellers 141
Discount cards 83, 143
Divadlo Archa 72
*Don Giovanni* (Mozart) 73,
74
marionette 64
Dorotheum 80
DOX Centre for
Contemporary Art 54,
130
Drahomíra 61
Dripstone Wall 65
Driving 139
Drowned Man 60
Drugs 142
Dubček, Alexander 11
Dukla Memorial 30
Dům u Minuty 28
Dürer, Albrecht 41
Dvořák, Antonín 57
Dvořák Museum 122

**E**
Easter Monday 85
Eccentric Prague 64–5
Electricity supply 140
Elevator (Old Town Hall)
30
Emergency numbers 142
Emmaus Devil 61
Entertainment *see*
Performing arts venues
Erpet Bohemia Crystal 80,
92
Estates Theatre 73, 74
Etiquette 143
European Union 11
Experiences 12–13

**F**
Family attractions 70–71
Fantova Kavárna 68–9
Fashion 116
Ferdinand II 25
Festivals 84–5

Film 69, 84
Folimanka Underground Bunker 65
Folk tales 61
Food and drink 12, 13, 76–7
 budget tips 83
 shops 116
 *see also* Bars and pubs; Beer; Cafés; Kavárnas; Restaurants
Franciscan Garden 43, 65, 119, 121
Free attractions 82–3
Funicular (Petřín Hill) 47

**G**

Galerie Mánes 121, 122
Galerie Via Art 122
Gallery of Steel Figures 64
Gans, David 38
Garrigue, Tomáš 25
Gehry, Frank 120
Germanic tribes 8
Ghosts and Legends Museum 60
Ghost tours 65, 74
Gift shops 71, 81, 101
Glass 80, 92, 101, 116
Golden Horseshoe 59
Golden Key 58
Golden Lane 23, 61
Golden Portal (St Vitus Cathedral) 26
Golden Tiger 59
Golden Wheel 58
Golem, The 60
Gothic Cellars (Old Town Hall) 30
Gothic Chapel (Old Town Hall) 30
Government advice 140
Grand Café Orient 79, 94
Grand Hotel Europa 43
Greater Prague 126–33
 cafés and pubs 132
 hotels 147
 itineraries 129
 map 126–7
 restaurants 133
 sights 127–31
 Vyšehrad sights 131

Great South Tower (St Vitus Cathedral) 26
Grebovka 69
Green Lobster 59
Green, The (Old Town Hall) 30
Guttmann, Robert 36

**H**

Habsburg dynasty 9, 10
Hašek, Jaroslav 56, 57
Havelské Tržiště 81
Havel, Václav 11, 25, 57
Health 142
Hemingway Bar 79, 93
Heydrich, Reinhard 53
Heydrich Terror Memorial 53
High Altar (St Vitus Cathedral) 26
High Synagogue 115
Hilsner, Leopold 39
Historical sites 52–3
Historic buildings
 Cubist Houses (Vyšehrad) 131
 Dům u Minuty 28
 Fantova Kavárna 68–9
 Golden Horseshoe 59
 Golden Key 58
 Golden Tiger 59
 Golden Wheel 58
 Grand Hotel Europa 43
 Green Lobster 59
 Hotel International 69
 House at the Stone Bell 28
 Jewish Town Hall 115
 Malá Strana Bridge Tower 33
 Municipal House (Obnecní dům) 52–3, 89, 91
 New Town Hall 120
 Old Town Bridge Tower 32, 52
 Old Town Hall 30, 91
 Petřín Tower 52
 Powder Gate 52, 89, 91
 Red Lamb 58
 Štorch House 29, 59
 Three Fiddles 59
 Two Suns 58

Historic buildings (cont)
 Villa Müller 130
 White Swan 58
History 8–11
Hitler, Adolf 10–11
Holešovice 127
Holocaust 36, 39
Holy Roman Empire 8, 9
Hostels 83
Hotel International 69
Hotels
 Greater Prague 147
 Malá Strana 145
 Nové Město 146–7
 Prague Castle and Hradčany 145–6
 Staré Město 144–5
House at the Stone Bell 28
House signs 58–9
Hrabal, Bohumil 57
Hračky U Zlatého lva 71, 80, 92
Hradčanské náměstí 107
Hradčany *see* Prague Castle and Hradčany
Hunger Wall 47
Husák, Gustáv 25
Hus, Jan 9, 29, 85, 91
Hussite Wars 9, 25
Hybernia 72

**I**

Ice hockey 13
ID 143
Idiom 65
Immigration 11
Independence Day 85
Inner Courtyard (Loreta) 34–5
Insurance 141
Iron Man 60
Itineraries
 2 Days 14–15
 4 Days 16–17
 Greater Prague 129
 Josefov and Northern Staré Město 115
 Malá Strana 99
 Nové Město 121

Itineraries (cont)
  Prague Castle and
    Hradčany 107
  Staré Město 91

**J**

Jaffe, Mordechai ben
  Abraham 20
Jan Hus Day 85
Jan Hus Memorial 29
Jazz 75, 93
Jerusalem Synagogue 121
Jewellery 80, 92, 101, 116
Jewish community 39
  Jewish Ghetto 8, 39
  Jewish leaders 39
  Jewish Museum **36–9**, 55
  Jewish Town Hall 115
  pogroms 9, 39
  World War II 11, 36
  *see also* Synagogues
Jewish Museum **36–9**, 55
Jewish Town Hall 115
John Lennon Wall 82, 97,
  99
John of Luxemburg 8–9,
  31
Josefov and Northern Staré
  Město 112–17
  cafés and restaurants
    117
  itinerary 115
  map 112–13
  shopping 116
  sights 113–15

**K**

Kafka, Franz 39, 56, 57
  grave 130
Kampa Island 64, 98, 99
Kara, Avigdor 38
Karel Zeman Museum 69
Karlova 91
Karlovy Vary International
  Film Festival 84
Kaunitz Palace 100
Kavárnas 78–9, 108, 124,
  132
Kenton's 79, 93
Kepler, Johannes 90
Kinský Palace 29
Kinský Summer Palace 47

Klausen Synagogue 36, 38,
  114, 115
Krymská 69
Kundera, Milan 57
Kunsthalle Praha 55
Kutná Hora 90

**l**

Labour Day 85
Lamppost, Cubist 68
Landau, David ben Yehuda
  39
Language 141
  essential phrases 140
  phrase book 156–7
Lapidárium 130
Legátová, Květa 57
Lego Museum 71, 122
Letná 83
Letná Park 128
Liechtenstein Palace 100
Literature 56–7, 85
Lobkowicz Palace 22, 100,
  108
Local Artists Praha 81
Loew ben Bezalel, Rabbi
  Judah 38, 39, 60, 114
Loos, Alfred 130
Loreta **34–5**, 50, 106, 107
Loretánské náměstí 34,
  107
Lorraine Cross (Charles
  Bridge) 32
Louis Wing (Old Royal
  Palace) 24
Lunch 83

**M**

McGee's Ghost Tours 65,
  74
Mácha, Karel Hynek 47
Mad Barber 61
Maisel, Mordechai 38, 39,
  114, 115
Maisel Synagogue 37, 114,
  115
Malá Strana 96–103
  cafés and pubs 102
  hotels 145
  itinerary 99
  map 96
  palaces 100

Malá Strana (cont)
  restaurants 103
  shopping 101
  sights 97–100
Malá Strana Bridge Tower
  33
Malé náměstí 29
Malostranské náměstí 33
Maltézské náměstí 98
Manufaktura 81, 92
Marian Column 29
Marionettes 64, 70, 71, 73
Markets 80–81
  Havelské Tržiště 81
  Náplavka Farmers'
    Market 81
*Martyrdom of St Florian*
  (Altdorfer) 41
Masaryk, Jan 61
Masaryk, Tomáš 10, 39
Masopust 84
May Day 84
Memorials
  Communist Memorial
    42–3
  Dukla Memorial 30
  Heydrich Terror Memorial
    53
  Jan Hus Memorial 29
  National Memorial on the
    Vitkov Hill 53, 129
  Slavín Monument
    (Vyšehrad) 131
  Wall of Commemoration
    (Pinkas Synagogue) 36
  White Mountain
    Memorial 30
Metro 138
Michna Palace 100
Mikuláš of Kadaň 31
Miluláš Vánoce, Silvestr 85
Milunic, Vlado 120
Mirror Chapel
  (Clementinum) 73, 90
Mirror Maze (Petřín Hill) 47,
  71
Mobile phones 143
Monasteries and convents
  Břevnov Monastery 130
  St Agnes of Bohemia
    Convent **40–41**, 73,
    115

Monasteries and convents (cont)
St George's Convent (Prague Castle) 22–3
Strahov Monastery 47
*see also* Churches and cathedrals
Money 141
Morzin Palace 100
Mozart, Wolfgang Amadeus 64, 73, 74, 98
Mucha, Alfons 57
Mucha Museum 122
Munich Agreement 11
Municipal Hall (Old Town Hall) 30
Municipal House (Obnecní dům) 52–3, 89, 91
Museums and galleries 54–5
Bel Art Gallery 101
Bílek Villa 130
City of Prague Museum 54–5, 130
Cold War Museum 43
DOX Centre for Contemporary Art 54, 130
Dvořák Museum 122
Galerie Mánes 121, 122
Galerie Via Art 122
Gallery of Steel Figures 64
Ghosts and Legends Museum 60
Jewish Museum **36–9**, 55
Karel Zeman Museum 69
Kunsthalle Praha 55
Lapidárium 130
Lego Museum 71, 122
Mucha Museum 122
Museum of Communism 121, 122
Museum of Decorative Arts 55
Museum of Senses 64, 122
Museum of Torture 65
Muzeum Slivovice R. Jelínek 101

Museums and galleries (cont)
National Gallery 40–41, 54
National Museum 42, **44–5**, 54, 122
National Museum of Agriculture 130
National Technical Museum 55, 70
Police Museum 122
Public Transport Museum 70
Railway Kingdom 71
Robert Guttmann Gallery 36
Sex Machines Museum 65
Smetana Museum 54
Václav Špála Gallery 122
Music 56–7, 72–3
budget tips 83
festivals 84
live 75, 93
Myths and legends 60–61

**N**

Náplavka 69
Náplavka Farmers' Market 81
Na Příkopě 119
National Gallery 40–41, 54
National Holidays 85
National Library 90
National Marionette Theatre 64, 70, 73
National Memorial on the Vitkov Hill 53, 129
National Museum 42, **44–5**, 54, 122
National Museum of Agriculture 130
National Technical Museum 55, 70
National Theatre 72, 74, 120, 121
Nature reserves, Divoká Šárka 69
Nazi regime 10–11, 39, 53
Němcová, Božena 56, 57
Nerudova 97, 99

New Archbishop's Chapel (St Vitus Cathedral) 27
New Castle Steps 106, 107
New Stage 72
New Town Hall 120
Nightlife 74–5
Nové Město 123
Staré Město 93
Nostitz Palace 100
Nové Město 118–25
cafés and pubs 124
hotels 146–7
itinerary 121
map 118
museums and galleries 122
nightlife 123
restaurants 125
sights 119–22
Nový Svět 106, 107
Nusle Bridge (Vyšehrad) 131

**O**

Observation Tower (Petřín Hill) 46
Off the Beaten Track 66–7
Old Castle Steps 106–7
Old Jewish Cemetery 37, 38, 82, 113, 115
Old Land Rolls Room (Old Royal Palace) 24
Old-New Synagogue 37, 50, 114–15
Old Royal Palace 22, 24, 25
Old Town Bridge Tower 32, 52
Old Town Hall 30, 91
Old Town Square **28–31**, 89, 91
Olšany Cemetery 130
One-Armed Thief 60
Opening hours 141
Oppenheim, Rabbi David ben Abraham 38, 39
Ottokar II 25
Our Lady before Týn, Church of 28–9, 51
Our Lady of the Mangles 33
Our Lady of the Snows, Church of 43
Our Lady Victorious, Church of 50, 99

**P**

Palace Gardens Below
    Prague Castle 65
Palaces
    Buquoy Palace 100
    Černín Palace 107
    Kaunitz Palace 100
    Kinský Palace 29
    Kinský Summer Palace
        47
    Liechtenstein Palace
        100
    Lobkowicz Palace 22, 100,
        108
    Michna Palace 100
    Morzin Palace 100
    Nostitz Palace 100
    Old Royal Palace 22, 24,
        25
    Rosenberg Palace
        (Prague Castle) 23
    Schönborn Palace 100
    Schwarzenberg Palace
        107
    Sternberg Palace 54, 105,
        107
    Thun-Hohenstein Palace
        100
    Troja Château 129
    Wallenstein Palace 97,
        100
Palach, Jan 43, 45, 130
Palackého náměstí 121
Palác Koruna 43
Palác Lucerna 43, 68
Pantheon (National
    Museum) 44
Parking 139
Parks and gardens 13,
    64–5
    Botanical Garden of
        Charles University 82
    Botanical Garden Troja
        70–71
    DinoPark 70
    Franciscan Garden 43, 65,
        119, 121
    The Green (Old Town
        Hall) 30
    Kampa Island 64, 98,
        99
    Letná Park 128

Parks and gardens (cont)
    Palace Gardens Below
        Prague Castle 65
    Petřín Hill **46–7**, 64, 97
    Prague Castle Grounds
        82
    Prague Castle Royal
        Garden 65
    Riegrovy sady 69
    Royal Garden 105
    South Gardens (Prague
        Castle) 22, 65
    Stromovka 65, 128, 129
    Vojanovy sady 83, 99
    Vrtba Garden 64, 99
    Vyšehrad 64
    Wallenstein Garden 65,
        83, 97, 99
    *see also* Nature reserves
Parléř, Petr 24
Passports 140
Pavel, Petr 25
Performing arts venues
    Black Light Theatre 71
    Divadlo Archa 72
    Estates Theatre 73, 74
    Hybernia 72
    National Marionette
        Theatre 64, 70, 73
    National Theatre 72, 74,
        120, 121
    New Stage 72
    Ponec 72
    Rudolfinum 73
    Smetana Hall 72
    State Opera 72, 120
    *see also* Festivals
Personal security 142
Petřín Hill **46–7**, 64, 97
Petřín Tower 52
Phrase book 156–7
Pinkas Synagogue 36, 51,
    114, 115
Pivovarský dům 79
Police 142
    Police Museum 122
Ponec 72
Porcelain 92
Postal services 143
Powder Gate 52, 89, 91
Prague Castle **22–5**, 105,
    107

Prague Castle Grounds 82
Prague Castle and
    Hradčany 104–9
    cafés and pubs 108
    hotels 145–6
    itinerary 107
    map 104–5
Prague Castle and
    Hradčany (cont)
    restaurants 109
    sights 105–7
Prague Castle Royal Garden
    65
Prague Metronome on
    Letná Plinth 53
Prague Spring 10, 11
Prague Spring International
    Music Festival 84
Prague Sun (Loreta) 35
Prague Writer's Festival
    85
Prague Zoo 70, 127, 129
Pragulic 64
Přemyslid dynasty 8
Prices
    average daily spend
        140
    public transport 136
Public transport 83,
    137–8
    prices 136
Public Transport Museum
    70
Pubs *see* Bars and pubs
Puchner Altarpiece (St
    Agnes of Bohemia
    Convent) 41
Puppet shows 64, 70, 73

**R**

Railway Kingdom 71
Rapoport, Solomon Judah
    Lieb 39
Red Lamb 58
Reformation 9
Refugees, Ukrainian 11
Refunds 143
Religion 61
Renewal of the
    Independent Czech State
    85
Responsible tourism 143

Restaurants
  budget tips 83
  Greater Prague 133
  Josefov and Northern
    Staré Město 117
  Malá Strana 103
  Nové Město 125
  Petřín Hill 46
Restaurants (cont)
  Prague Castle and
    Hradčany 109
  Staré Město 29, 95
  Wenceslas Square 42
Rettigová, M D 57
Riders' Staircase (Old Royal
  Palace) 24
Riegrovy sady 69
Robert Guttmann Gallery
  36
Rosenberg Palace (Prague
  Castle) 23
Rotunda of St Martin
  (Vyšehrad) 129, 131
Royal Crypt (St Vitus
  Cathedral) 26
Royal Garden 105
Royal Oratory (St Vitus
  Cathedral) 27
Rudolf II 25
Rudolfinum 73
Rulers 25
Rules of the road 136, 139

**S**

Safety
  government advice 140
  personal security 142
Santa Casa (Loreta) 34,
  35
Schönborn Palace 100
Schwarzenberg Palace
  107
Sex Machines Museum 65
Shopping 80–81
  for children 71
  Josefov and Northern
    Staré Město 116
  Malá Strana 101
  Staré Město 92
Sidon, Efraim Karol 39
Sigismund (St Vitus
  Cathedral) 27

Signal Festival 85
Sir Nicholas Winton Statue
  53
Slavín Monument
  (Vyšehrad) 131
Slavs 8
*Slivovice* 101
Slovaks 61
Smetana, Bedřich 54, 56–7,
  127
  grave 131
  Smetana Museum 54
Smetana Hall 72
Smoking 142
Soběslav Residence (Old
  Royal Palace) 24
Socialist-Realist
  architecture 69
Solomon ben Aaron of
  Lunshits, Ephraim 39
South Gardens (Prague
  Castle) 22, 65
Souvenir shops 71, 81, 92
Soviet era 10, 11, 42–3, 45
  architecture 69
Spanish Synagogue 37, 51,
  73, 113, 115, 116
Specific requirements,
  travellers with 141
Speed limits 136
Stag Moat 106
St Agnes of Bohemia 41
St Agnes of Bohemia
  Convent **40–41**, 73, 115
Staré Město 88–95
  cafés and pubs 84
  hotels 144–5
  itinerary 91
  map 88–9
  nightlife 93
  restaurants 95
  shopping 92
  sights 89–91
  *see also* Josefov and
    Northern Staré Město
State Opera 72, 120
Statues, Charles Bridge
  32–3
St Cajetan Church 73
Štefánik's Observatory 47
Sternberg Palace 54, 105,
  107

St George's Basilica (Prague
  Castle) 23, 73
St George's Convent
  (Prague Castle) 22–3
St John of Nepomuk 61
  statue 32
  tomb 27
St Lawrence, Church of
  47
St Luitgard 33
St Martin in the Wall 73
St Nicholas Cathedral 29,
  73, 91
St Nicholas Church Malá
  Strana 50, 73, 98, 99
Štorch House 29, 59
Story of Prague 8–11
Story of Prague Castle
  (exhibition) 24
Strahov Monastery 47
Strahov Stadium 46
Strakonice Madonna 40
Street Theatre Festival
  84
Stromovka 65, 128, 129
Sts Cyril and Methodius
  Cathedral of 51, 119,
    121
  Cyril and Methodius Day
    85
  statue 32
Sts Peter and Paul
  Cathedral (Vyšehrad)
    131
Sts Simon and Jude, Church
  of 73
St Vitus Cathedral **26–7**, 50,
  105, 107
St Wenceslas's Horse
  (mural) 59
St Wilgefortis Altar (Loreta)
  35
Světlá, Karolína 56
Synagogues
  etiquette 143
  High Synagogue 115
  Jerusalem Synagogue
    121
  Klausen Synagogue 36,
    38, 114, 115
  Maisel Synagogue 37,
    114, 115

Old-New Synagogue 37, 50, 114–15
Pinkas Synagogue 36, 51, 114, 115
Spanish Synagogue 37, 51, 73, 113, 115, 116

**T**
Tábor Gate (Vyšehrad) 129, 131
Tanec Praha 84
Tap Water 142
Taxes 143
Taxis 83, 138
Theatres see Performing arts venues
Theodoricus, Master 41
Thirty Years' War 9, 25
Three Fiddles 59
Thun-Hohenstein Palace 100
Tickets, public transport 137
Time Zone 142
Tomb of St John of Nepomuk (St Vitus Cathedral) 27
Toy shops 71, 80, 92, 101
Trade Fair Palace 54
Train travel 136–7
Trams 138
Travel
    getting around 136–9
    government advice 140
Travel passes 83, 143
Treasury (Loreta) 35
Třeboň Altarpiece (St Agnes of Bohemia Convent) 41
Trinitarian Order 33
Troja Château 129
Turk in Ungelt 60
Two Suns 58

**U**
U Fleků 78, 121, 124
Ungelt 29, 90, 91
U Tří Růží 79, 94
U Zlatého tygra 78, 91, 94

**V**
Vaccinations 141
Václav Havel Airport Prague 136
Václav Špála Gallery 122

VAT 143
Velhartice Altarpiece (St Agnes of Bohemia Convent) 41
Velvet Revolution 10, 11, 41, 61
Viewing Gallery (Old Town Hall) 30
View points 12, 83
Villa Müller 130
Vinohrady 127, 129
Visas 140
Vladislav Hall (Old Royal Palace) 24, 25
Vladislav II 25
Vltava, River 61
    boat trips 71, 75, 138
Vojanovy sady 83, 99
Vrtba Garden 64, 99
Vyšehrad 64, 127, 129, 131
Vyšehrad Castle 52, 61, 127
Vyšehrad Cemetery 82
Vyšší Brod Altarpiece (St Agnes of Bohemia Convent) 40
Výstaviště 128, 129

**W**
Walking 139
    tours 82–3, 139
Wall of Commemoration (Pinkas Synagogue) 36, 114, 115
Wallenstein Garden 65, 83, 97, 99
Wallenstein Palace 97, 100
Wenceslas 25
    statues 42, 43, 68, 121
Wenceslas Chapel (St Vitus Cathedral) 27
Wenceslas IV 25
Wenceslas Square 15, 17, **42–3**, 119, 121
Werewolf 61
White Mountain, Battle of 9, 25
White Mountain Memorial 30
White Swan 58

White Tower (Prague Castle) 22
Wi-Fi 143
Wildlife, Prague Zoo 70, 127, 129
Winton, Sir Nicholas 53
World War II 10–11, 39, 53, 65

**Z**
Zbraslav Madonna 40
Želivský, Jan 43
Zemach, Mordecai 38
Zeman, Karel 69
Žižkov 128, 129
Žižkov TV Tower 53, 128, 129

# PHRASE BOOK

## In an Emergency

| | | |
|---|---|---|
| Help! | Pomoc! | po-mots |
| Stop! | Zastavte! | zas-tav-te |
| Call a doctor! | Zavolejte doktora! | za-vo-ley-te dok-to-ra! |
| Call an ambulance! | Zavolejte sanitku! | za-vo-ley-te sa-nit-ku! |
| Call the police! | Zavolejte policii! | za-vo-ley-te poli-tsi-yi! |
| Call the fire brigade! | Zavolejte hasiče | za-vo-ley-te ha-si-che |
| Where is the telephone? | Kde je telefon? | gde ye te-le-fohn? |
| the nearest hospital? | nejbližší nemocnice? | ney-blizh-shee ne-mo-tsnyi-tse? |

## Communication Essentials

| | | |
|---|---|---|
| Yes/No | Ano/Ne | ano/ne |
| Please | Prosím | pro-seem |
| Thank you | Děkuji vám | dye-ku-ji vahm |
| Excuse me | Prosím vás | pro-seem vahs |
| Hello | Dobrý den | do-bree den |
| Goodbye | Na shledanou | na shle-da-nou |
| Good evening | Dobrý večer | do-bree ve-cher |
| morning | ráno | rah-no |
| afternoon | odpoledne | od-po-led-ne |
| evening | večer | ve-cher |
| yesterday | včera | vche-ra |
| today | dnes | dnes |
| tomorrow | zítra | zee-tra |
| here | tady | ta-di |
| there | tam | tam |
| What? | Co? | tso? |
| When? | Kdy? | gdi? |
| Why? | Proč? | proch? |
| Where? | Kde? | gde? |

## Useful Phrases

| | | |
|---|---|---|
| How are you? | Jak se máte? | yak se mah-te? |
| Very well, thank you. | Velmi dobře děkuji | vel-mi do-brze dye-ku-yi |
| Pleased to meet you | Těší mě | tye-shee mnye |
| See you soon | Uvidíme se brzy | u-vi-dyee-me-se brzy |
| That's fine | To je v pořádku | to ye vpo-rzhahdku |
| Where is/are...? | Kde je/jsou ...? | gde ye/ysou ...? |
| How long does it take to get to...? | Jak dlouho to trvá se dostat do...? | yak dlou-ho to tr-vah se dos-tat ...? |
| How do I get to...? | Jak se dostanu k ...? | yak se dos-ta-nuh k...? |
| Do you speak English? | Mluvíte anglicky? | mlu-vee-te an-glits-ki? |
| I don't understand | Nerozumím | ne-ro-zu-meem |
| Could you speak more slowly? | Mohl(a)* byste mluvit trochu pomaleji? | mo-hl(a) bys-te mlu-vit tro-khu po-ma-ley? |
| Pardon? | Prosím? | pro-seem? |
| I'm lost | Ztratil(a)* jsem se | stra-tyil (a) ysem se |

## Sightseeing

| | | |
|---|---|---|
| art gallery | galerie | ga-le-ri-ye |
| bus stop | autobusová zastávka | au-to-bus-o-vah za-stah-vka |
| church | kostel | kos-tel |
| garden | zahrada | za-hra-da |
| library | knihovna | knyi-hov-na |
| museum | muzeum | mu-ze-um |
| railway station | nádraží | nah-dra-zhee |
| tourist information | turistické informace | tu-ris-tits-ke in-for-ma-tse |
| closed for the public holiday | státní svátek | staht-nyee svah-tek |

## Shopping

| | | |
|---|---|---|
| How much does this cost? | Co to stojí? | tso to sto-yee? |
| I would like... | Chtěl(a)* bych... | khtyel(a) bikh... |
| Do you have...? | Máte...? | maa-te ...? |
| I'm just looking | Jenom se dívám | ye-nom se dyee-vahm |
| Do you take credit cards? | Berete kreditní karty? | be-re-te kre-dit –nyee kar-ti? |
| What time do you open/close? | V kolik otevíráte/ zavíráte? | v ko-lik o-te-vee-rah-te/ za-vee-rah-te? |
| this one | tento | ten-to |
| that one | tamten | tam-ten |
| expensive | drahý | dra-hee |
| cheap | levný | lev-nee |
| size | velikost | ve-li-kost |
| white | bílý | bee-lee |
| black | černý | cher-nee |
| red | červený | cher-ve-nee |
| yellow | žlutý | zhlu-tee |
| green | zelený | ze-le-nee |
| blue | modrý | mod-ree |
| brown | hnědý | hnye-dee |

## Types of Shop

| | | |
|---|---|---|
| antique shop | starožitnictví | sta-ro zhit— |
| bank | banka | ban-ka |
| bakery | pekárna | pe-kahr-na |
| bookstore | knihkupectví | knih-kupets-tvee |
| butcher | řeznictví | rzhez-nyits-tvee |
| chemist (prescriptions etc) | lékárna | leh-kahr-na |
| chemist (toiletries etc) | drogerie | dro-ge-riye |
| delicatessen | lahůdky | la-hood-ki |
| department store | obchodní dům | op-khod-nyee doom |
| grocery | potraviny | po-tra-vi-ni |
| glass | sklo | sklo |
| market | trh | trh |
| post office | pošta | posh-ta |
| supermarket | samoobsluha | sa-mo-ob-slu-ha |
| tobacconist | tabák | ta-bahk |
| travel agency | cestovní kancelář | tses-tov-nyi kan-tse-laarzh |

## Staying in a Hotel

| | | |
|---|---|---|
| Do you have a vacant room? | Máte volný pokoj? | mah-te vol-nee po-koy? |
| double room | dvoulůžkový pokoj | dvou-loozh-ko-vee po-koy |

| with double bed | s dvojitou postelí | s dvoy-tou pos-te-lee |
| twin room | pokoj s dvěma postelemi | po-koy sdvye-ma pos-te-le-mi |
| porter | vrátný | vrah-tnee |
| key | klíč | kleech l |
| have a reservation | Mám reservaci | mahm re-zer-va-tsi |

## Eating Out

| Have you got a table for…? | Máte stůl pro …? | mah-te stool pro …? |
| I'd like to reserve a table | Chtěl(a)* bych rezervovat stůl | khtyel(a) bikh re-zer-vo-vat stool |
| breakfast | snídaně | snyee-danye |
| lunch | oběd | ob-yed |
| dinner | večeře | ve-che-rzhe |
| The bill, please | Prosím, účet | pro-seem oo-chet |
| I am a vegetarian | Jsem vegetarián (ka)* | ysem veghe-tariahn(ka) |
| waitress! | slečno | slech-no |
| waiter! | pane vrchní! | pane vrkh-nyee! |
| fixed-price menu | standardní menu | stan-dard-nyee menu |
| dish of the day | nabídka dne | na-beed-ka dne |
| starter | předkrm | przhed-krm |
| main course | hlavní jídlo | hlav-nyee yeed-lo |
| vegetables | zelenina | ze-le-nyi-na |
| dessert | zákusek | zah-kusek |
| cover charge | poplatek | pop-la-tek |
| wine list | nápojový lístek | nah-po-yo-vee lees-tek |
| rare (steak) | krvavý | kr-va-vee |
| medium | středně udělaný | strzhed-nye u-dye-la-nee |
| well done | dobře udělaný | dobrzhe- u-dye-la-nee |
| glass | sklenice | sklen-yitse |
| bottle | láhev | lah-hev |
| knife | nůž | noozh |
| fork | vidlička | vid-lich-ka |
| spoon | lžíce | lzhee-tse |

## Menu Decoder

| biftek | bif-tek | steak |
| bílé víno | bee-leh vee-no | white wine |
| bramborové knedlíky | bram-bo-ro-veh kne-dleeki | potato dumplings |
| brambory | bram-bo-ri | potatoes |
| chléb | khlehb | bread |
| cukr | tsukr | sugar |
| čaj | chay | tea |
| červené víno | cher-ven-eh vee-no | red wine |
| grilované | gril-ov-a-neh | grilled |
| houskové knedlíky | ho-sko-veh kne-dleeki | bread dumplings |
| hovězí | hov-ye-zee | beef |
| hranolky | hra-nol-ki | chips |
| husa | hu-sa | goose |
| jablko | ya-bl-ko | apple |
| jehněčí | ye-hnye-chee | lamb |
| kachna | kakh-na | duck |
| kapr | ka-pr | carp |
| káva | kah-va | coffee |
| kuře | ku-rzhe | chicken |
| kyselé zelí | kis-el-eh zel-ee | sauerkraut |
| maso | ma-so | meat |
| máslo | mah-slo | butter |

| mléko | mleh-ko | milk |
| mořská jídla | morzh-skah yeed-la | seafood |
| párek | paa-rek | sausage |
| pečený | petsh-en-eh | baked |
| pečené | pech-en-eh | roast |
| polévka | po-lehv-ka | soup |
| pivo | pi-vo | beer |
| ryba | ri-ba | fish |
| rýže | ree-zhe | rice |
| salát | sa-laat/sa-laht | salad |
| sůl | sool | salt |
| sýr | seer | cheese |
| šunka | shun-ka | ham |
| vařená/ uzená | va-rzhe-nah u-zenah | cooked smoked |
| telecí | te-le-tsee | veal |
| vajíčko | va-yeech-ko | egg |
| vařené | va-rzhe-neh | boiled |
| vepřové | vep-rzho-veh | pork |
| voda | vo-da | water |
| zelenina | ze-le-nyi-na | vegetables |

## Numbers

| 1 | jedna | yed-na |
| 2 | dvě | dvye |
| 3 | tř | trzhi |
| 4 | čtyři | chti-rzhi |
| 5 | pět | pyet |
| 6 | šest | shest |
| 7 | sedm | sedm |
| 8 | osm | osm |
| 9 | devět | dev-yet |
| 10 | deset | de-set |
| 11 | jedenáct | ye-de-nahtst |
| 12 | dvanáct | dva-nahtst |
| 13 | třináct | trzhi-nahtst |
| 14 | čtrnáct | chtr-nahtst |
| 15 | patnáct | pat-nahtst |
| 16 | šestnáct | shest-nahtst |
| 17 | sedmnáct | sedm-nahtst |
| 18 | osmnáct | osm-nahtst |
| 19 | devatenáct | de-va-te-nahtst |
| 20 | dvacet | dva-tset |
| 21 | dvacet jedna | dva-tset yed-na |
| 22 | dvacet dva | dva-tset dva |
| 30 | třicet | trzhi-tset |
| 40 | čtyřicet | chti-rzhi-tset |
| 50 | padesát | pa-de-saht |
| 60 | šedesát | she-de-saht |
| 70 | sedmdesát | sedm-de-saht |
| 80 | osmdesát | osm-de-saht |
| 90 | devadesát | de-va-de-saht |
| 100 | sto | sto |
| 1,000 | tisíc | tyi-seets |
| 2,000 | dva tisíce | dva tyi-see-tse |
| 5,000 | pět tisíc | pyet tyi-seets |
| 1,000,000 | milión | mi-li-ohn |

## Time

| one minute | jedna minuta | yed-na mi-nu-ta |
| one hour | jedna hodina | yed-na ho-dyi-na |
| half an hour | půl hodiny | pool ho-dyi-ni |
| day | den | den |
| week | týden | tee-den |
| Monday | pondělí | pon-dye-lee |
| Tuesday | úterý | oo-te-ree |
| Wednesday | středa | strzhe-da |
| Thursday | čtvrtek | chtvr-tek |
| Friday | pátek | pah-tek |
| Saturday | sobota | so-bo-ta |
| Sunday | neděle | ned-yel-e |

# ACKNOWLEDGMENTS

## This edition updated by

**Contributors** Mark Baker, Joesph Reaney

**Senior Editor** Alison McGill

**Project Editor** Charlie Baker

**Senior Designers** Laura O'Brien, Stuti Tiwari

**Art Editor** Bandana Paul

**Editor** Vineet Singh

**Proofreader** Ben Ffrancon Dowds

**Indexer** Helen Peters

**Picture Research Manager** Taiyaba Khatoon

**Senior Picture Researcher** Nishwan Rasool

**Picture Research Team** Priya Singh, Manpreet Kaur, Samrajkumar.S

**Publishing Assistant** Simona Velikova

**Jacket Designer** Laura O'Brien

**Senior Cartographer** Subhashree Bharati

**Senior Cartographic Editor** James Macdonald

**Cartography Manager** Suresh Kumar

**Senior DTP Designer** Tanveer Zaidi

**DTP Designer** Rohit Rojal

**Senior Production Manager** Balwant Singh

**Image Retouching-Production Manager** Pankaj Sharma

**Production Controller** Kariss Ainsworth

**Managing Editors** Beverly Smart, Hollie Teague

**Managing Art Editor** Gemma Doyle

**Senior Managing Art Editor** Priyanka Thakur

**Art Director** Maxine Pedliham

**Publishing Director** Georgina Dee

DK would like to thank the following for their contribution to the previous editions: Hilary Bird, Demetrio Carrasco, John Coletti, Paul Franklin, Kathryn Glendenning, Nancy Mikula, Rough Guides/Angus Osborn, Rough Guides/ Susannah Sayler, Jonathan Schultz, Tony Souter, Linda Whitwam.

The publisher would like to thank the following for their kind permission to reproduce their photographs:

(Key: a-above; b-below/bottom; c-centre; f-far; l-left; r-right; t-top)

**Alamy Stock Photo:** Andrey Akimov 66b, Album 54, Belikart 63tr, Carlo Bollo 9br, Petr Bonek 8, Ian Bottle 59b, Peter Forsberg / CR 47b, © Zdenek Pridal / CTK Photo 93b, CTK 10bl, 56b, CTK Photo / Katerina Sulova 12cr, Katerina Sulova / CTK Photo 93t, Ian Dagnall 89t, Britta Pedersen / dpa 11, dpa picture alliance 57, Robert Dziewulski 23bl, Adam Eastland 13bl, eFesenko, 26cla, GL Archive 9tl, Manfred Glueck 72, Shim Harno 56t, Rieger Bertrand / Hemis.fr 15tl, Historic Images 41cla, Home Bird 77b, imageBROKER / Moritz Wolf 98, imageBROKER. com GmbH & Co. KG / Walter G. Allgöwer 33cla, Images&Stories 21cla, INTERFOTO / History 61, Ivoha 52t, kaprik 127t, Brenda Kean 105t, John Kellerman 68t, Vitalii Kliuiev 13cl, Art Kowalsky 44-45b, Loop Images Ltd / Anna Stowe 83t, MB_ Photo 114-115t, Hercules Milas 24, MiraMira 101, Jim Monk 106t, John Norman 38b, Cum Okolo 12br, 13cl (8), 15br, 40b, 60t, 73, 74t, 92, 95, 103, 121b, PBarchive 25, 39, J. Pie 111br, 124t, PjrStatues 111bl, PjrTravel 10clb, 59t, 90t, Peter Forsberg / Praha 128, Prisma Archivo 9cr, Mieneke Andeweg-van Rijn 62-63, Shawshots 10cla, Charles Stirling (Travel) 71, stockex 13cla, Lana Sundman 31, Liba Taylor 84, Maksym Tsalko 30, Steve Tulley 13clb, Lucas Vallecillos 75t, volkerpreusser 124b, Mike Withers 64b, Yegorovnick 67t, Zoonar / Kai Michael Neuhold 53t.

**Aromi:** 133.

**Artel Glass:** 81t.

**Bakeshop Praha:** 116.

**Depositphotos Inc:** VividaPhoto 113t.

**Dorling Kindersley:** Jiri Kopriva 122, Vladimir Kozlik 58b, Frantisek Preucil 114b, Stanislav Tereba 82.

**Dreamstime.com:** Anton Aleksenko 14, 52b, Sorin Colac 34br, Dziewul 26b, Anton Eine 76t, Evgeniy Fesenko 34-35t, 37b, Veronika Galkina 16crb, Marian Garai 131, Diego Grandi 23br, 65, Grounder 106-107b, Natalia Hanin 44cla, Nataliya Hora 97t, Josefkubes 33tc, Kaprik 66t, Zoran Kompar 21ca, Madeleinesteinbach 81b, Kirill Makarov 51t, Marietf 20cla, Andres Garcia Martin 90b, Roman Milert 37t, Mistervlad 28b, Martin Molcan 12cra, Montypeter 85, Luciano Mortula 21cr, Marketa Novakova 130, Positivetravelart 74-75b, Nikita Pritykin 70, Pytyczech 6-7, 17, 99tl, Dietmar Rauscher 78t, Pavel Rezac 87, Rumata7 97b, Vladimir Sazonov 120, Jozef Sedmak 63cra, Josef Skacel 129b, Stevanovicigor 9tr, 50b, Stockfotocz 7 6b, Jana Telenská 77t, Thecriss 119b, Anibal Trejo 23crb, Uko_jesita 33tr, Wrangel 80b, Yakub88 27t.

**Getty Images:** Hulton Archive / Keystone / Stringer 10br, imageBROKER / Silwen Randebrock 49, Moment / Alexander Spatari 19, 28-29t, Moment / Andrey Denisyuk 119t, Moment / Karl Hendon 135.

**Getty Images / iStock:** alexxx_77 12crb, Bim 22-23t, E+ / borchee 5, E+ / Eloi_Omella 32-33b, kiiiiiin 47t, Roman Kybus 42bl, PytyCzech 46, serge001 42-43t.

**Grand Café Orient:** Jaroslav Turek 79.

**Hotel U Prince:** 94.

**John Lennon Pub:** 102.

**Karel Zeman Museum:** 69.

**King Solomon Restaurant:** 117.

**Kuchyň:** 109.

**Lobkowicz Palace Museum:** Lobkowicz Palace Café, Prague Castle Complex, Prague, Czech Republic 108.

**Loreto Sanctuary:** 35bc.

**National Technical Museum:** 55b.

**Nebe Cocktail & Music Bar:** 123.

**Prague Spring Festival:** Ivan Maly 83b.

**Restaurace Pastička:** 132.

**Shutterstock.com:** Belikart 113br, Marina Datsenko 110-111t, hsunny 13tl, KievVictor 29br, PhotoFires 41tr, tichr 60b, Popova Valeriya 100, Sergio Delle Vedove 51b.

**U Šumavy:** 125.

### Cover images:
*Front and Spine:* **Dreamstime.com:** Emicristea; *Back:* **Alamy Stock Photo:** Robert Dziewulski tr; **Dreamstime.com:** Veronika Galkina tl; **Getty Images / iStock:** E+ / borchee cl.

### Sheet Map Image:
**Dreamstime.com:** Emicristea.

All other images © Dorling Kindersley Limited
For further information see: www.dkimages.com
**Illustrator:** Chris Orr & Associates

First edition 2003

Published in Great Britain by Dorling Kindersley Limited,
DK, One Embassy Gardens, 8 Viaduct Gardens,
London SW11 7BW, UK

The authorised representative in the EEA is
Dorling Kindersley Verlag GmbH. Arnulfstr.
124, 80636 Munich, Germany

Published in the United States by DK Publishing,
1745 Broadway, 20th Floor, New York, NY 10019, USA

A CIP catalog record for this book
is available from the British Library.

A catalog record for this book is available
from the Library of Congress.

ISSN: 1479-344X
ISBN: 978-0-2416-7671-4

Printed and bound in China

www.dk.com

**MIX**
Paper | Supporting
responsible forestry
FSC™ C018179

This book was made with Forest
Stewardship Council™ certified
paper – one small step in DK's
commitment to a sustainable future.
Learn more at **www.dk.com/uk/
information/sustainability**